A Journey through Genesis

The 50 Day Bible Challenge

Edited by Marek P. Zabriskie

FORWARD MOVEMENT
Cincinnati, Ohio

A Journey through Genesis

The 50 Day Bible Challenge

Library of Congress Control Number: 2023935775

#2666

ISBN: 978-088028-521-6

Printed in USA

www.forwardmovement.org

Dedicated to Charles Zabriskie Jr.,
my father,
who has been the genesis of
much that is good in the world,
in our family, and in the church,
and has equipped his sons for life.

Preface

The Bible Challenge began as a simple idea in 2011: to encourage daily reading of scripture. Simple ideas can bring forth great change. Since then, over a million people have participated across the Anglican Communion.

Developing a daily spiritual discipline or practice is crucial for all Christians who wish to be faithful followers of Jesus. Saint Augustine and many other great Christians have written about the power of reading the Bible quietly on our own. There is no other book in the world that can so transform the human heart, motivate the human spirit, and give us the mind that was in Christ Jesus himself.

The Bible remains the world's best-selling book year after year. However, Episcopalians, Roman Catholics, and other mainline Christians often do not read it. Yet, studies show that prayerfully engaging scripture is the best way for Christians to grow in their faith and love of Jesus. For our churches to grow and our members to deepen their spiritual lives, we must devote time each day to engaging God's Word.

The goal of The Bible Challenge is to help individuals develop a lifelong, daily spiritual discipline of reading the Bible so that their lives may be constantly transformed and renewed. Hundreds of thousands of people around the world have taken on the Bible Challenge. The series includes a yearlong study of the Bible, and the Bible Challenge Gospel Series: reading each book (Matthew, Mark, Luke, and John) over a 50-day period. In addition, thematic Bible Challenge books offer a way for readers to go deep into scripture to learn what God is saying on a particular subject. The Social Justice

Bible Challenge builds upon the hunger to engage in scripture and connects our desire to help with God's mandate to love and serve others. The Way of Love Bible Challenge explores seven core spiritual practices through the lens of scripture. And the Creation Care Bible Challenge calls us back into relationship with God the Creator of all creation.

Regular engagement with the Bible develops a strong Christian faith, enhances our experience of worship, and helps each of us to become a more committed, articulate, and contagious Christian. This is exactly what the world needs today.

With prayers and blessings for your faithful Bible reading,

The Rev. Marek P. Zabriskie
Founder of The Bible Challenge
Director of the Center for Biblical Studies
www.thecenterforbiblicalstudies.org
Rector of Christ Church Greenwich, Connecticut

How to Read the Bible Prayerfully

Welcome to a journey with Genesis. We are delighted that you are interested in reading God's life-transforming Word. It will change and enrich your life. This book is an ideal resource for individuals, small groups, churches, and dioceses. Here are some suggestions to consider as you get started:

- You can begin your journey with Genesis at any time of year. Since it's the first book of the Bible, some people may want to start the new year with a new practice of daily scripture reading. With 50 meditations, the book is a perfect companion for the 50 days in the season of Easter—or the 40 days (plus Sundays) of Lent. Reading and reflecting on the Bible is a year-long, day-in, day-out endeavor, and the book can be read at any period.

- Each day has a manageable amount of reading, a meditation, a few questions, and a prayer, written by a host of wonderful authors.

- We suggest that you try to read the Bible each day. This is a great spiritual discipline to establish.

- If you need more than fifty days to read through *A Journey through Genesis*, move at the pace that works best for you.

- Many Bible Challenge participants read the Bible using their iPad, iPhone, Kindle, or Nook, or listen to the Bible on a mobile device using Audio.com, faithcomesthroughhearing.org, or Pandora radio. Find what works for you.

- Other resources for learning more about the Bible and engaging scripture can be found on our website at www.ForwardMovement.org. In addition, you can find a list of resources at www.thecenterforbiblicalresources.org. The center also offers a Read the Bible in a Year program and reading plans for the New Testament, Psalms, and Proverbs in a Year.

- Because the Bible is not a newspaper, it is best to read it with a reverent spirit. We advocate a devotional approach to reading the Bible, rather than reading it as a purely intellectual or academic exercise.

- Before reading the Bible, take a moment of silence to put yourself in the presence of God. We then invite you to read this prayer written by Archbishop Thomas Cranmer.

    Blessed Lord, who has caused all holy scriptures to be written for our learning: Grant us to hear them, read, mark, learn, and inwardly digest them, that we may embrace and ever hold fast the blessed hope of everlasting life, which you have given us in our Savior Jesus Christ; who lives and reigns with you and the Holy Spirit, one God, for ever and ever. Amen.

- Consider using the ancient monastic practice of *lectio divina*. In this form of Bible reading, you read the text and then meditate on a portion of it, be it a verse or two or even a single word. Mull over the words and their meaning. Then offer a prayer to God based on what you have read, how it has made you feel, or what it has caused you to ponder. Listen in silence for God to respond to your prayer.

- We encourage you to read in the morning, if possible, so that your prayerful reading may spiritually enliven the rest of your day. If you cannot read in the morning, read when you can later in the day. Try to carve out a regular time for your daily reading.

- One way to hold yourself accountable to reading God's Word is to form a group within your church or community, particularly any outreach and ministry groups. By participating in the Genesis Bible Challenge together, you can support one another in your reading, discuss the Bible passages, ask questions, and share how God's Word is transforming your life.

- Ask to have a notice printed in your church newsletter that you are starting a group to read and study *A Journey through Genesis*. Invite others to join you and gather regularly to discuss the readings, ask questions, and share how they transform your life. Visit the Center for Biblical Resources website to see more suggestions about how churches can participate in The Bible Challenge.

- Have fun and find spiritual peace and the joy that God desires for you in your daily reading. The Center for Biblical Studies aims to help you discover God's wisdom and to create a lifelong spiritual practice of daily Bible reading so that God may guide you through each day of your life.

- Once you've finished one complete reading of the Bible, start over and do it again. God may speak differently to you in each reading. Follow the example of U.S. President

John Adams, who read through the Bible each year during his adult life. We highly advocate this practice.

- After participating in The Genesis Bible Challenge, you will be more equipped to support and mentor others in reading the Bible—and to connect your ministry of advocacy and assistance with Holy Scripture.

We are thrilled that you are participating in The Bible Challenge. May God richly bless you as you prayerfully engage the scriptures each day. To learn more about The Bible Challenge, visit us at: www.thecenterforbiblicalstudies.org to see all of our resources.

Introduction to the book of Genesis

Perhaps no book in the Bible offers more powerful, riveting, intriguing, and at times disturbing stories than the book of Genesis. Indeed, Genesis qualifies for great literature. Some of the stories told within it transcend the Bible and have become part of our vernacular, for churched and unchurched folks alike. For instance, the stories of Adam and Eve, Cain and Abel, Noah's Ark, the Tower of Babel, and Joseph and his brothers are well known in both secular and religious circles.

The name genesis means "origin" or "birth" in ancient Greek. In the Hebrew Bible (the *Tanakh*) the book of Genesis is known as *Bereshith*, taken from the opening line, "In the beginning…" Genesis is part of the Torah, the first five books of the Old Testament, also called the Pentateuch, taken from the Greek word for "five books."

Traditionally, authorship of the Torah or Pentateuch was ascribed to Moses. This belief carried into the New Testament (see Luke 24:27). But the book of Genesis also refers to events that take place after Moses's life, such as when the Canaanites were no longer in the land (Genesis 12:6). And the fifth book of the Torah, Deuteronomy, refers to Moses's death and burial; obviously Moses would find it difficult to write about his death, which led scholars to conclude a different source for authorship.

Today, scholars believe Genesis was written by several writers known as "J," "E," and "P," which stand for the Yahwistic source (J for Jahwist in German), the Elohist (these writings are identified by the name that they use for God, "Yahweh" or "Elohim"), and finally, the Priestly Writer. Each writer had his own style, theology, and story to tell. Their combined works were then redacted or edited into one cohesive work after a long history of being kept alive in both written and oral tradition.

Genesis was written over many centuries. Most scholars believe Genesis was composed in the tenth century after the establishment of the monarchy in Israel. Many important parts of Genesis, however, were not written until after the fall of the monarchy in 586 BCE, when Nebuchadnezzar's troops swept down from the north to sack Jerusalem. The invaders took many of the inhabitants of Jerusalem captive and marched them to Babylon.

It is important to recognize at the outset that Genesis contains folk tales, legends, and myths. Legends are not lies. We should not dismiss the truth of these tales, for legends and myths were ways of transmitting truth in the ancient world. These stories precede any understanding of science as we know it. Hence, we must suspend our scientifically trained minds to encounter Genesis on its own grounds as a collection of stories that illuminate life.

The stories of these characters are vital not only to Jews and Christians, but also with the advent of Islam in the sixth century, the Quran features stories of Adam and Eve, Abraham and Ishmael (who is said to be the father of all Muslims), and Joseph. In the Quran, it is Ishmael, not Isaac, who Abraham nearly sacrificed to God (Genesis 22). Hence, the three major Abrahamic religions share a common reverence for the stories of Genesis.

We are told that God created the universe. For believers, this truth still holds. There is an intelligent design of sorts to all that we see and know. People of faith do not have to believe that the world was created in six days or that God used a flood to destroy the earth.

No man or woman was present at creation. Hence, reading Genesis should never be confused with reading a newspaper. Instead, Christians have traditionally read Genesis metaphorically and allegorically.

The story of Adam and Eve conveys a vital truth, namely that God created humans and intended for them to prosper and experience joy, but humans violated boundaries set by God and were held accountable. When we violate the boundaries that God has established, we face consequences, not because God is vindictive, but because we have violated the protections that God has provided to keep us safe.

The Bible is a strange book full of very human stories. The best and worst of humanity is depicted within its covers. It tells the story of how God made a covenant with an individual named Abraham, whose children become a family and then a tribe, then a collection of tribes, and finally a nation. Genesis and the Torah are the story of the Jewish people. But Genesis begins by examining the advent of humanity at large and the interplay of God and humans.

The first eleven chapters of Genesis constitute primeval history. They are divided up into stories about the first humans (Genesis 1:1-6:4) and the flood and dispersal of humanity following the flood (Genesis 6:5-11:9). Chapters 1-11 offer archetypes of humanity found in Adam and Eve, Cain and Abel, Noah and the Flood, the Tower of Babel, and Joseph and his brothers.

In chapters 12-50, we switch from the wide-angel lens of primeval history to a narrow focus on ancestral history, examining Abraham and Sarah (chapters 12-25), Jacob and Esau (chapters 26-36), and Joseph and his brothers (chapters 37-50). The role of the ancient matriarchs—Sarah, Rebekah, Rachel, and Leah—also play a vital role in carrying out the fulfillment of God's promises. Along the way, we move from the urge for fratricide (Genesis 4:1-16; 27:41-45, 33:12-17) to full reunion when Joseph reconciles with his brothers who sold him into slavery.

Embedded in Genesis is the story of God's covenant that begins with Noah, who is given a sign of this covenant in a rainbow, and is officially established with Abraham, who is to become the father of the Jewish people with more descendants than stars in the sky.

The Bible itself begins in a garden (the Garden of Eden) and ends in a city (the City of God depicted in the book of Revelation). Early on, Adam and Eve are flung out of Paradise, and the Bible becomes the story of Paradise Regained, when Jesus offers himself on the cross to reconcile humanity with God.

God created the world, but human sin mars God's creation. Nevertheless, the overall message of Genesis and the Torah is a hopeful one. God is in charge and is watching over humankind. God intervenes when humans make a mess of their lives and seeks to bring about good from even the most difficult situations.

Ultimately, Genesis is part of a much bigger story. We need to read the entire Torah (or, as Gerhard von Rad would argue, the entire Hexateuch—the Torah and the book of Joshua) in order to understand what Genesis is trying to communicate. Many of these stories were aetiologies, meant to explain the facts of tribal history, about a place. They are episodes of country life. They take place at springs and watering holes, inside bed chambers and at work sites. All of these wondrous stories are meant to convey that God is with us, working to reconcile us.

A Journey through Genesis

The 50 Day Bible Challenge

Genesis 1

1 In the beginning when God created the heavens and the earth, ²the earth was a formless void and darkness covered the face of the deep, while a wind from God swept over the face of the waters.

³Then God said, "Let there be light"; and there was light. ⁴And God saw that the light was good; and God separated the light from the darkness. ⁵God called the light Day, and the darkness he called Night. And there was evening and there was morning, the first day.

⁶And God said, "Let there be a dome in the midst of the waters, and let it separate the waters from the waters." ⁷So God made the dome and separated the waters that were under the dome from the waters that were above the dome. And it was so.

⁸God called the dome Sky. And there was evening and there was morning, the second day.

⁹And God said, "Let the waters under the sky be gathered together into one place, and let the dry land appear." And it was so. ¹⁰God called the dry land Earth, and the waters that were gathered together he called Seas. And God saw that it was good. ¹¹Then God said, "Let the earth put forth vegetation: plants yielding seed, and fruit trees of every kind on earth that bear fruit with the seed in it." And it was so. ¹²The earth brought forth vegetation: plants yielding seed of every kind, and trees of every kind bearing fruit with the seed in it. And God saw that it was good. ¹³And there was evening and there was morning, the third day.

¹⁴And God said, "Let there be lights in the dome of the sky to separate the day from the night; and let them be for signs and for seasons and for days and years, ¹⁵and let them be lights in the dome of the sky to give light upon the earth." And it was so. ¹⁶God made the two great lights—the greater light to rule the day and the lesser light to rule the night—and the stars. ¹⁷God set them in the dome of the sky to give light upon the earth, ¹⁸to rule over the day and over the night, and to separate the light from the darkness. And God saw that it was good. ¹⁹And there was evening and there was morning, the fourth day.

²⁰And God said, "Let the waters bring forth swarms of living creatures, and let birds fly above the earth across the dome of the sky." ²¹So God created the great sea monsters and every living creature that moves, of every kind, with which the waters swarm, and every winged bird of every kind. And God saw that it was good. ²²God blessed them, saying, "Be fruitful and multiply and fill the waters in the seas, and let birds multiply on the earth." ²³And there was evening and there was morning, the fifth day.

²⁴And God said, "Let the earth bring forth living creatures of every kind: cattle and creeping things and wild animals of the earth of every kind." And it was so. ²⁵God made the wild animals of the earth of every kind, and the cattle of every kind, and everything that creeps upon the ground of every kind. And God saw that it was good.

²⁶Then God said, "Let us make humankind in our image, according to our likeness; and let them have dominion over the fish of the sea, and over the birds of the air, and over the cattle, and over all the wild animals of the earth, and

over every creeping thing that creeps upon the earth." [27]So God created humankind in his image, in the image of God he created them; male and female he created them. [28]God blessed them, and God said to them, "Be fruitful and multiply, and fill the earth and subdue it; and have dominion over the fish of the sea and over the birds of the air and over every living thing that moves upon the earth."

[29]God said, "See, I have given you every plant yielding seed that is upon the face of all the earth, and every tree with seed in its fruit; you shall have them for food. [30]And to every beast of the earth, and to every bird of the air, and to everything that creeps on the earth, everything that has the breath of life, I have given every green plant for food." And it was so.

[31]God saw everything that he had made, and indeed, it was very good. And there was evening and there was morning, the sixth day.

Reflection

According to the Jewish tradition, God authored the original Hebrew scroll of the Torah, the Five Books of Moses. Each Hebrew word, syllable, and letter within the Torah is considered *Lashon Kodesh* or Holy Language.

The first Hebrew word in the Torah is *B'reisheet*. "In the beginning" begins with the letter *bet*. The last word in the Torah is *Yisrael*; "Israel" ends with the letter *lahmed*. Together, these two Hebrew letters spell the word *lehv*, which means heart, and this is understood to teach that God provided Torah to humanity as an act of divine love.

In chapter one, Genesis notes how God ordered Creation with divine purpose. Genesis 1:7 teaches that God "made the dome and separated the waters that were under the dome from the waters that were above the dome." The Torah is like water. Just as water sustains and nurtures physical life, Torah study sustains and promotes our spiritual lives and gives us the inspiration by which we seek God's purpose in our lives.

Genesis 1:27 notes that God created the human being *B'tzelem Elohim*—in God's image. Judaism asserts three primary teachings on *B'tzelem Elohim*:

1. All life is sacred and must be protected.
2. No human is inherently more important than another.
3. Although we may look different from one another, the infinite nature of the Divine means that we are all equally created in the image of God.

Every single human life is precious and equal. Within our too often contentious world, we forget the inherent divine equality between all of us. We indulge in the sin of thinking "I am more important" than another and subsequently permit our behaviors to reflect this denial of our intrinsic human equality.

If we could all continually look at the "stranger's face" and see our equal, we would demand that all people receive universal support such as food, shelter, clothing, education, medical care, etc. God's intention is for us to look in everyone else's faces and see God and manifest God's love. To embrace God's purpose, we must continually strive to combat hate and violence within our community, nation, and world and actively pursue love and peace.

— **Rabbi Mitchell M. Hurvitz**

Questions_____

When can you see God's image in others' faces?

When is it more difficult for you to see the image of God in other people?

How can the responsibility of being created *B'Tzelem Elohim* help inform our choices?

Prayer _____

God, each of us is created equally in your divine image. Our sacred obligation is to treat everyone with the respect and love you manifest for us. Help us to recognize within everyone your spark of the divine and treat them with as much respect, blessing, and welcome as we would in our love for you. May we be worthy of your sacred intention and love for us. *Amen.*

Genesis 2

2 Thus the heavens and the earth were finished, and all their multitude. ²And on the seventh day God finished the work that he had done, and he rested on the seventh day from all the work that he had done. ³So God blessed the seventh day and hallowed it, because on it God rested from all the work that he had done in creation. ⁴These are the generations of the heavens and the earth when they were created. In the day that the LORD God made the earth and the heavens, ⁵when no plant of the field was yet in the earth and no herb of the field had yet sprung up—for the LORD God had not caused it to rain upon the earth, and there was no one to till the ground; ⁶but a stream would rise from the earth, and water the whole face of the ground— ⁷then the LORD God formed man from the dust of the ground, and breathed into his nostrils the breath of life; and the man became a living being.

⁸And the LORD God planted a garden in Eden, in the east; and there he put the man whom he had formed. ⁹Out of the ground the LORD God made to grow every tree that is pleasant to the sight and good for food, the tree of life also in the midst of the garden, and the tree of the knowledge of good and evil. ¹⁰A river flows out of Eden to water the garden, and from there it divides and becomes four branches. ¹¹The name of the first is Pishon; it is the one that flows around the whole land of Havilah, where there is gold; ¹²and the gold of that land is good; bdellium and onyx stone

are there. ¹³The name of the second river is Gihon; it is the one that flows around the whole land of Cush. ¹⁴The name of the third river is Tigris, which flows east of Assyria. And the fourth river is the Euphrates. ¹⁵The LORD God took the man and put him in the garden of Eden to till it and keep it.

¹⁶And the LORD God commanded the man, "You may freely eat of every tree of the garden; ¹⁷but of the tree of the knowledge of good and evil you shall not eat, for in the day that you eat of it you shall die."

¹⁸Then the LORD God said, "It is not good that the man should be alone; I will make him a helper as his partner." ¹⁹So out of the ground the LORD God formed every animal of the field and every bird of the air, and brought them to the man to see what he would call them; and whatever the man called every living creature, that was its name. ²⁰The man gave names to all cattle, and to the birds of the air, and to every animal of the field; but for the man there was not found a helper as his partner.

²¹So the LORD God caused a deep sleep to fall upon the man, and he slept; then he took one of his ribs and closed up its place with flesh. ²²And the rib that the LORD God had taken from the man he made into a woman and brought her to the man. ²³Then the man said, "This at last is bone of my bones and flesh of my flesh; this one shall be called Woman, for out of Man this one was taken." ²⁴Therefore a man leaves his father and his mother and clings to his wife, and they become one flesh. ²⁵And the man and his wife were both naked, and were not ashamed.

Reflection

The first chapter of Genesis refers to God as *Elohim*, whereas chapter two uses the title of *Yahweh-Elohim*. These Hebrew names for God indicate God's actions through two distinct divine attributes. *Elohim* is characteristic of God's justice and *Yahweh*, God's mercy.

"In the beginning," according to the Jewish tradition, God intended to create the world solely based on the divine attribute of justice. But God quickly realized that such a world would not survive. Thus, God gave precedence to the divine attribute of mercy and allied it with the quality of justice.

God is like a parent. We must follow God's divine instructions because this is how we lead sacred lives. But, like children who know a parent's expectations, we can fall short and disappoint. Subsequently, God's love and mercy are more evident than God's justice.

Also, because God created us equally in the divine image, we emphasize mercy over justice within our human interactions with each other. When we act with the priority of mercy, we more easily fulfill God's commandments to love our neighbor and the stranger in our midst.

A famous ancient rabbinic legend tells of Rabbi Meir traveling on a road where there were hooligans. One afternoon, his wife, Beruria, heard him pray that these wicked men should die. Beruria challenged her husband: "Would it not be better to pray that these evil men should change their ways?" Rabbi Meir learned from Beruria the true meaning of prioritizing mercy over justice. Mercy is the more powerful lever by which we can help cultivate others to change for the better.

Every individual desires justice against others but would prefer mercy be extended to themselves. God's love emphasizes mercy over justice because the divine intention is that we provide everyone the opportunity to grow and change for the better. God teaches us that the purpose of our lives is to love the "other" as we want to be loved. There is no more excellent ingredient to love than emphasizing mercy over justice.

We do not set aside justice, but we seek mitigation whenever possible. Our desire and emphasis on mercy guard us against going too far, and we create the love-filled world God intended "in the beginning."

— **Rabbi Mitchell M. Hurvitz**

Questions

When have you emphasized mercy over justice?

What mixture of mercy versus justice do you feel most matches God's will?

How do we cultivate our willingness to extend greater mercy to others, especially those we think might not deserve it?

Prayer

Merciful God, we pray to you for the strength to emphasize our mercy for others. Guide our hearts and hands to love as you love. Inspire us to live up to the divine ideals by which you created us in your image. May the knowledge of your love and mercy help us to bring peace to our lives. *Amen.*

Genesis 3

3 Now the serpent was more crafty than any other wild animal that the Lord God had made. He said to the woman, "Did God say, 'You shall not eat from any tree in the garden'?" ²The woman said to the serpent, "We may eat of the fruit of the trees in the garden; ³but God said, 'You shall not eat of the fruit of the tree that is in the middle of the garden, nor shall you touch it, or you shall die.'" ⁴But the serpent said to the woman, "You will not die; ⁵for God knows that when you eat of it your eyes will be opened, and you will be like God, knowing good and evil."

⁶So when the woman saw that the tree was good for food, and that it was a delight to the eyes, and that the tree was to be desired to make one wise, she took of its fruit and ate; and she also gave some to her husband, who was with her, and he ate. ⁷Then the eyes of both were opened, and they knew that they were naked; and they sewed fig leaves together and made loincloths for themselves. ⁸They heard the sound of the Lord God walking in the garden at the time of the evening breeze, and the man and his wife hid themselves from the presence of the Lord God among the trees of the garden.

⁹But the Lord God called to the man, and said to him, "Where are you?" ¹⁰He said, "I heard the sound of you in the garden, and I was afraid, because I was naked; and I hid myself."

¹¹He said, "Who told you that you were naked? Have you eaten from the tree of which I commanded you not to eat?" ¹²The man said, "The woman

whom you gave to be with me, she gave me fruit from the tree, and I ate." ¹³Then the Lord God said to the woman, "What is this that you have done?" The woman said, "The serpent tricked me, and I ate."

¹⁴The Lord God said to the serpent, "Because you have done this, cursed are you among all animals and among all wild creatures; upon your belly you shall go, and dust you shall eat all the days of your life. ¹⁵I will put enmity between you and the woman, and between your offspring and hers; he will strike your head, and you will strike his heel."

¹⁶To the woman he said, "I will greatly increase your pangs in childbearing; in pain you shall bring forth children, yet your desire shall be for your husband, and he shall rule over you."

¹⁷And to the man he said, "Because you have listened to the voice of your wife, and have eaten of the tree about which I commanded you, 'You shall not eat of it,' cursed is the ground because of you; in toil you shall eat of it all the days of your life; ¹⁸thorns and thistles it shall bring forth for you; and you shall eat the plants of the field. ¹⁹By the sweat of your face you shall eat bread until you return to the ground, for out of it you were taken; you are dust, and to dust you shall return."

²⁰The man named his wife Eve, because she was the mother of all living.

²¹And the Lord God made garments of skins for the man and for his wife, and clothed them.

²²Then the Lord God said, "See, the man has become like one of us, knowing good and evil; and now, he might reach out his hand and take also from the tree of life, and eat, and live forever"— ²³therefore the Lord God sent him forth

from the garden of Eden, to till the ground from which he was taken. ²⁴He drove out the man; and at the east of the garden of Eden he placed the cherubim, and a sword flaming and turning to guard the way to the tree of life.

Reflection

The world we live in is not as God originally intended it to be. God has mysteriously baked into creation the possibility of going awry from God's original plans and purposes, but this actually comes to pass not due to God but to our own free decision-making. Humanity has exiled itself from the perfect communion with God, which was our original glory, ushering in consequences not just for us but for all creation—pain and death foremost among them.

All this is embedded in the second creation myth in Genesis, told through the incredible drama of Eve's temptation, Adam's assent, God's curses on the serpent, the woman, and the man, and humanity's expulsion from the verdant garden in which we were once in God's personal company. Theological truths are told here in the language of a story.

The narrative can make God's acts seem arbitrary, even capricious: God has put in the garden a desirable tree only to forbid eating of it; God curses our first parents when they transgress this prohibition and banishes them from the garden so that they won't eat of the tree of life and gain immortality as well as the knowledge of good and evil; and so on.

Many of the early church fathers, though, interpreted the curses that befall our first parents in the narrative more as organic consequences of their actions rather than as juridical punishments doled out by God. Athanasius, for example, says that God made humankind mortal, capable of dying, but intended us originally to share in the grace and power of God's own life and so live forever. But we forsook this lifegiving communion with God, and so reverted to our natural, mortal state. The punishment of life without God is life without God. This is what life east of Eden means.

The mystery of the Fall opens the door for chaos to rush into creation, even into our human hearts, minds, and bodies. But we need not lose heart. The Bible begins with our forsaking Eden. It ends with God bringing us back to it (Revelation 22:1-5).

— **The Rev. Dr. Justin E. Crisp**

Questions

Where have you felt the effects of the Fall most acutely: in bodily or mental illness, for example, in difficulty knowing what is the right thing to do, or in difficulty *doing* what you know is the right thing to do?

Deception and mistrust are integral to the story of the Fall: the serpent lies to Eve, and she acquiesces to the serpent's suggestion that God hasn't been completely forthcoming with her and Adam about the forbidden tree. How might God be calling you to trust his promises to you rather than give them up for some other, sham promise of security or happiness?

Prayer

Lord God, you made us for yourself, to share your company and partake of your own life and goodness: we give you thanks that, when we gave ourselves reason to hide from you, you did not hide yourself from us, but persisted to love, shield, and restore us; through Jesus Christ our Lord. *Amen.*

Genesis 4

4 Now the man knew his wife Eve, and she conceived and bore Cain, saying, "I have produced a man with the help of the Lord." [2]Next she bore his brother Abel. Now Abel was a keeper of sheep, and Cain a tiller of the ground.

[3]In the course of time Cain brought to the Lord an offering of the fruit of the ground, [4]and Abel for his part brought of the firstlings of his flock, their fat portions. And the Lord had regard for Abel and his offering, [5]but for Cain and his offering he had no regard. So Cain was very angry, and his countenance fell.

[6]The Lord said to Cain, "Why are you angry, and why has your countenance fallen? [7]If you do well, will you not be accepted? And if you do not do well, sin is lurking at the door; its desire is for you, but you must master it."

[8]Cain said to his brother Abel, "Let us go out to the field." And when they were in the field, Cain rose up against his brother Abel, and killed him.

[9]Then the Lord said to Cain, "Where is your brother Abel?" He said, "I do not know; am I my brother's keeper?" [10]And the Lord said, "What have you done? Listen; your brother's blood is crying out to me from the ground! [11]And now you are cursed from the ground, which has opened its mouth to receive your brother's blood from your hand. [12]When you till the ground, it will no longer yield to you its strength; you will be a fugitive and a wanderer on the earth."

[13]Cain said to the Lord, "My punishment is greater than I can bear! [14]Today you have driven me away from the soil,

and I shall be hidden from your face; I shall be a fugitive and a wanderer on the earth, and anyone who meets me may kill me." ¹⁵Then the LORD said to him, "Not so! Whoever kills Cain will suffer a sevenfold vengeance." And the LORD put a mark on Cain, so that no one who came upon him would kill him.

¹⁶Then Cain went away from the presence of the LORD, and settled in the land of Nod, east of Eden. ¹⁷Cain knew his wife, and she conceived and bore Enoch; and he built a city, and named it Enoch after his son Enoch. ¹⁸To Enoch was born Irad; and Irad was the father of Mehujael, and Mehujael the father of Methushael, and Methushael the father of Lamech.

¹⁹Lamech took two wives; the name of the one was Adah, and the name of the other Zillah. ²⁰Adah bore Jabal; he was the ancestor of those who live in tents and have livestock. ²¹His brother's name was Jubal; he was the ancestor of all those who play the lyre and pipe. ²²Zillah bore Tubal-cain, who made all kinds of bronze and iron tools. The sister of Tubal-cain was Naamah.

²³Lamech said to his wives: "Adah and Zillah, hear my voice; you wives of Lamech, listen to what I say: I have killed a man for wounding me, a young man for striking me. ²⁴ If Cain is avenged sevenfold, truly Lamech seventy-sevenfold."

²⁵Adam knew his wife again, and she bore a son and named him Seth, for she said, "God has appointed for me another child instead of Abel, because Cain killed him." ²⁶To Seth also a son was born, and he named him Enosh. At that time people began to invoke the name of the LORD.

Reflection

Human history begins with banishment, and civilization is kicked off by murder. HBO has nothing on the Bible.

What takes place between Cain and Abel is all too human. Cain, the elder son of Adam and Eve, and Abel, the younger, both make sacrifices to God from the results of their labor. It's said that God "had regard for Abel and his offering," but not for Cain and his. The reason for this is unsaid. Regardless, Cain envies Abel his esteem in God's eyes and resolves to kill him. Cain murders Abel in a place of seclusion and tries to lie to God about it when confronted, but the ground itself testifies against Cain. Cain is exiled from God, east of Eden, where he and his descendants give birth to hallmarks of civilization, to cities, nomadic cultures, music and art, and metalworking. Good and noble as these may be, Cain's murderous streak lives on in his descendants, as Lamech ups the ante of violence and kills two men who have wounded him. To the other side of Cain's legacy and lineage is that of Seth, Adam and Eve's son after Abel, whose descendants are said to worship the Lord.

It's tempting to read the Bible as though it's a story about other people. But these two lineages, Cain's and Seth's, the line of murder and the line of love, run right through our world, and they run right through us—even what is best and most ingenious in and around us. Humankind is fragile after the Fall, and we are perennially tempted to shore up our fragility by resorting to violence and revenge. Jesus, cut down like a new Abel, puts a divine stop to the line of violence. Whereas Abel's blood cries out to God for recompense from the ground, Jesus's is "the sprinkled blood that speaks a better word than the blood of Abel" (Hebrews 12:24), the word of forgiveness. God refuses to play by the stratagems of Cain, refuses to avenge even himself. And it changes everything.

— The Rev. Dr. Justin E. Crisp

Questions _____

When have you felt drawn to respond to some pain, loss, hurt, or vulnerability in your life with violence or harm? What happened to prevent you from acting on this desire, or, if you did act, what "better word" do you hear once you see that harm in the light of Christ?

Murder is Cain's response to his envy of Abel. In what way is envy a force in your life and soul? What would it take for you to feel safe and secure enough to give up envy, and for what renewal of God's promises might you ask in prayer so you can do so?

Prayer _____

Lord Jesus, yours is the blood that speaks a better word than the blood of Abel: pardon us when we lose ourselves in the ways of the world and give us grace to follow you in the way of the cross, which is the way of life. *Amen.*

Genesis 5

5 This is the list of the descendants of Adam. When God created humankind, he made them in the likeness of God. ²Male and female he created them, and he blessed them and named them "Humankind" when they were created. ³When Adam had lived one hundred thirty years, he became the father of a son in his likeness, according to his image, and named him Seth. ⁴The days of Adam after he became the father of Seth were eight hundred years; and he had other sons and daughters. ⁵Thus all the days that Adam lived were nine hundred thirty years; and he died.

⁶When Seth had lived one hundred five years, he became the father of Enosh. ⁷Seth lived after the birth of Enosh eight hundred seven years, and had other sons and daughters. ⁸Thus all the days of Seth were nine hundred twelve years; and he died. ⁹When Enosh had lived ninety years, he became the father of Kenan. ¹⁰Enosh lived after the birth of Kenan eight hundred fifteen years, and had other sons and daughters. ¹¹Thus all the days of Enosh were nine hundred five years; and he died. ¹²When Kenan had lived seventy years, he became the father of Mahalalel. ¹³Kenan lived after the birth of Mahalalel eight hundred and forty years, and had other sons and daughters. ¹⁴Thus all the days of Kenan were nine hundred and ten years; and he died. ¹⁵When Mahalalel had lived sixty-five years, he became the father of Jared. ¹⁶Mahalalel lived after the birth of Jared eight hundred thirty years, and had other sons

and daughters. ¹⁷Thus all the days of Mahalalel were eight hundred ninety-five years; and he died. ¹⁸When Jared had lived one hundred sixty-two years he became the father of Enoch. ¹⁹Jared lived after the birth of Enoch eight hundred years, and had other sons and daughters. ²⁰Thus all the days of Jared were nine hundred sixty-two years; and he died.

²¹When Enoch had lived sixty-five years, he became the father of Methuselah. ²²Enoch walked with God after the birth of Methuselah three hundred years, and had other sons and daughters. ²³Thus all the days of Enoch were three hundred sixty-five years. ²⁴Enoch walked with God; then he was no more, because God took him.

²⁵When Methuselah had lived one hundred eighty-seven years, he became the father of Lamech. ²⁶Methuselah lived after the birth of Lamech seven hundred eighty-two years, and had other sons and daughters. ²⁷Thus all the days of Methuselah were nine hundred sixty-nine years; and he died.

²⁸When Lamech had lived one hundred eighty-two years, he became the father of a son; ²⁹he named him Noah, saying, "Out of the ground that the LORD has cursed this one shall bring us relief from our work and from the toil of our hands." ³⁰Lamech lived after the birth of Noah five hundred ninety-five years, and had other sons and daughters. ³¹Thus all the days of Lamech were seven hundred seventy-seven years; and he died. ³²After Noah was five hundred years old, Noah became the father of Shem, Ham, and Japheth.

Reflection

There is a stereotype about the boring parts of the Bible that they are "nothing but 'begats'" (to use the terminology of older translations): long lists of who was the father of whom, with no narrative interest or relevance to our lives today. And chapter 5 of Genesis is indisputably a list of "begats." As it states in the first verse: "This is the list of the descendants of Adam." The writer of Genesis wants to establish a clear link between Adam, the first human being, and the rest of the story being told in the book. The list begins with Adam and ends with Noah, who will be the main character of the next four chapters.

Whether any of the people named in Genesis 5 actually existed cannot be established—and is not particularly important. All of them are depicted as living for hundreds of years: in the case of Methuselah, almost a millennium, the longest-lived of all, whose name has become synonymous with great old age. The writer wants to impress us through this account of superhuman lifespans with the nearness of these first people to God (as the first verse also emphasizes, "When God created humankind, he made them in the likeness of God").

And yet the most enduring impression received from this list of "begats" is of a family line very like our own: a series of fathers and sons (unfortunately, we hear almost nothing about the women of this bloodline at this point, except in the references to "other sons and daughters"), one following the other for generations. We know nothing about their relationships, but after the catastrophic fratricide of the story of Cain and Abel in chapter 4, this unbroken family line establishes a reassuring sense of continuity.

The chapter ends with the appearance of Noah and with an echo of the story of the Fall in Genesis 3: when Lamech names his son, he says, "Out of the ground that the Lord has cursed this one shall bring us relief from our work and from the toil of our hands." The human race is learning to live in the world after Adam and Eve's expulsion from the garden, and this family, with its steady march of generations, is a source of hope.

— The Rev. Grace Pritchard Burson

Questions _____

Why do you think this chapter puts such emphasis on the unnaturally long lifespans of the first descendants of Adam? Would the world be a better place if people actually lived for seven, eight, nine hundred years? Does living longer indicate that a person is somehow more blessed?

A legend has formed around Enoch, who "walked with God," that he did not actually die (an experience shared, in the Old Testament, only with the prophet Elijah, whom God took up to heaven in a chariot of fire [2 Kings 2:11]). Yet, Enoch is only granted half to a third of the lifespan of his ancestors and descendants. Which would be better: to live nine hundred years, or to "walk with God" without experiencing death?

This whole chapter is a list of family relationships. How far back can you trace your family? Are your relationships a source of pride and joy or of conflict and confusion? How would it feel to believe that God's plan is dependent on the generations of your family?

Prayer _____

God of all our generations, you created the human race in your image and you long to bring us into your family. Bless all our families, those we are born into and those we find and build ourselves. May we honor your likeness in each other; may the ties of kinship reflect your will for our lives; and may we walk with you for all our days, be they many or few. *Amen.*

Genesis 6

6 When people began to multiply on the face of the ground, and daughters were born to them, ²the sons of God saw that they were fair; and they took wives for themselves of all that they chose.

³Then the Lord said, "My spirit shall not abide in mortals forever, for they are flesh; their days shall be one hundred twenty years."

⁴The Nephilim were on the earth in those days—and also afterward—when the sons of God went in to the daughters of humans, who bore children to them. These were the heroes that were of old, warriors of renown. ⁵The Lord saw that the wickedness of humankind was great in the earth, and that every inclination of the thoughts of their hearts was only evil continually.

⁶And the Lord was sorry that he had made humankind on the earth, and it grieved him to his heart. ⁷So the Lord said, "I will blot out from the earth the human beings I have created— people together with animals and creeping things and birds of the air, for I am sorry that I have made them."

⁸But Noah found favor in the sight of the Lord. ⁹These are the descendants of Noah. Noah was a righteous man, blameless in his generation; Noah walked with God. ¹⁰And Noah had three sons, Shem, Ham, and Japheth.

¹¹Now the earth was corrupt in God's sight, and the earth was filled with violence. ¹²And God saw that the earth was corrupt; for all flesh had corrupted its ways upon the earth.

[13]And God said to Noah, "I have determined to make an end of all flesh, for the earth is filled with violence because of them; now I am going to destroy them along with the earth. [14]Make yourself an ark of cypress wood; make rooms in the ark, and cover it inside and out with pitch. [15]This is how you are to make it: the length of the ark three hundred cubits, its width fifty cubits, and its height thirty cubits. [16]Make a roof for the ark, and finish it to a cubit above; and put the door of the ark in its side; make it with lower, second, and third decks. [17]For my part, I am going to bring a flood of waters on the earth, to destroy from under heaven all flesh in which is the breath of life; everything that is on the earth shall die. [18]But I will establish my covenant with you; and you shall come into the ark, you, your sons, your wife, and your sons' wives with you. [19]And of every living thing, of all flesh, you shall bring two of every kind into the ark, to keep them alive with you; they shall be male and female. [20]Of the birds according to their kinds, and of the animals according to their kinds, of every creeping thing of the ground according to its kind, two of every kind shall come in to you, to keep them alive. [21]Also take with you every kind of food that is eaten, and store it up; and it shall serve as food for you and for them." [22]Noah did this; he did all that God commanded him.

Reflection

This chapter is definitely a candidate for weirdest chapter in the Bible, especially the first five verses that refer to mysterious "sons of God" having sexual relationships with human women, who then bore children who became "the heroes that were of old, warriors of renown." This theme is then promptly dropped, never to be referred to again, as the story of Noah and the Ark begins. Along the way, God also restricts the lifespan of mortals, who had previously lived multiple centuries, to a mere 120 years.

The rest of the chapter is on much more familiar ground, known to us from innumerable children's Bible story books. But of course, the story of Noah is much more disturbing than cheerful picture books full of pairs of animals indicate. God regrets creating humankind and laments their wickedness and decides to wipe them off the face of the earth, except for Noah, who has found favor in God's sight.

In Genesis chapter 6, the narrative takes the first definite steps out of the realm of myth— humans who live for eight hundred years, "sons of God" who breed with human women—into the realm of history. The narrative of the great flood is almost certainly indicative of a cultural memory of a regional inundation in the ancient Near East that caused massive destruction and loss of life.

This transition from myth to history will not be complete until the books of Samuel, when we encounter the first biblical characters who can definitively be said to have existed. But the story of Noah, situated as it is in the genre of myth, nevertheless has roots in real events and offers many resonances with our lives today. In the age of climate change, this tale of rising seas and endangered animals strikes us with new relevance. At a church conference on the religious response to the ecological crisis, we sang new words to the old gospel song, "We are climbing Jacob's ladder": *We are saving Noah's cargo.*

— **The Rev. Grace Pritchard Burson**

Questions _____

Do you agree with God's assessment in verse 5 that "the wickedness of humankind was great in the earth, and that every inclination of the thoughts of their hearts was only evil continually"?

What does it mean for God to be "sorry" that God has made human beings? Can God make bad decisions? Can God change God's mind?

Noah, apparently unquestioningly, obeys God's command to make the ark. Why do you think he does so? In his situation, would you have done the same?

Prayer _____

Forgiving God, your heart breaks at the hurt that human beings inflict on each other and on your good creation. May we, like Noah, find favor in your sight and resist the corruption and violence that infect the earth. As our generation faces new global challenges, show us the way forward that accords with your gracious will. *Amen*.

Genesis 7

7 Then the LORD said to Noah, "Go into the ark, you and all your household, for I have seen that you alone are righteous before me in this generation. ²Take with you seven pairs of all clean animals, the male and its mate; and a pair of the animals that are not clean, the male and its mate; ³and seven pairs of the birds of the air also, male and female, to keep their kind alive on the face of all the earth. ⁴For in seven days I will send rain on the earth for forty days and forty nights; and every living thing that I have made I will blot out from the face of the ground."

⁵And Noah did all that the LORD had commanded him. ⁶Noah was six hundred years old when the flood of waters came on the earth. ⁷And Noah with his sons and his wife and his sons' wives went into the ark to escape the waters of the flood. ⁸Of clean animals, and of animals that are not clean, and of birds, and of everything that creeps on the ground, ⁹two and two, male and female, went into the ark with Noah, as God had commanded Noah. ¹⁰And after seven days the waters of the flood came on the earth.

¹¹In the six hundredth year of Noah's life, in the second month, on the seventeenth day of the month, on that day all the fountains of the great deep burst forth, and the windows of the heavens were opened. ¹²The rain fell on the earth forty days and forty nights.

¹³On the very same day Noah with his sons, Shem and Ham and Japheth, and Noah's wife and the three wives of his sons entered the ark, ¹⁴they and every

wild animal of every kind, and all domestic animals of every kind, and every creeping thing that creeps on the earth, and every bird of every kind—every bird, every winged creature. ¹⁵They went into the ark with Noah, two and two of all flesh in which there was the breath of life. ¹⁶And those that entered, male and female of all flesh, went in as God had commanded him; and the LORD shut him in.

¹⁷The flood continued forty days on the earth; and the waters increased, and bore up the ark, and it rose high above the earth. ¹⁸The waters swelled and increased greatly on the earth; and the ark floated on the face of the waters. ¹⁹The waters swelled so mightily on the earth

that all the high mountains under the whole heaven were covered; ²⁰the waters swelled above the mountains, covering them fifteen cubits deep.

²¹And all flesh died that moved on the earth, birds, domestic animals, wild animals, all swarming creatures that swarm on the earth, and all human beings; ²²everything on dry land in whose nostrils was the breath of life died. ²³He blotted out every living thing that was on the face of the ground, human beings and animals and creeping things and birds of the air; they were blotted out from the earth. Only Noah was left, and those that were with him in the ark. ²⁴And the waters swelled on the earth for one hundred fifty days.

Reflection

This description of Noah and the flood may bring to mind for contemporary readers the rising sea levels and floods associated with climate change. This ancient story of humankind gone so wrong that God nearly wipes the slate clean to start over seems, on the one hand, unfathomably harsh, and, on the other hand, understandable. Don't we all sometimes look at the world and wonder what it would take fundamentally to clean up the mess humans have made?

The flood is a kind of deep cleansing or purging—a reboot—of the world. But God doesn't start over from scratch. He sees the integrity and righteousness of Noah and tells Noah to take into the ark a range of biodiversity with animals of all sorts and kinds. This family and these animals will be the seeds of a new humanity and a new creation.

This is no small storm. It is a deluge that drowns everything and everyone not in the ark. God is heartbroken over what humans have done. Yet God chooses a few to work through for the sake of many, which is a deep biblical pattern. Over and over again in scripture, God identifies, claims, and calls a few people to embody God's promises to many. This pattern reaches its most profound expression in the life, death, and resurrection of Jesus. In Jesus, God's profound love for humanity leads God to enter into and identify with the human condition at the most intimate level. God suffers with us in order to save and free us.

As we look around us at human-made disasters, it's tempting to fall into despair. Yet God has not abandoned us in the messes we have made. God is actively calling ordinary people like Noah—or you and me—into the work of helping to repair creation and human community. Sometimes this means waiting patiently through long seasons of storms.

— **The Rev. Dr. Dwight Zscheile**

Questions

What are some ways in which you might pay closer attention to God's call in your life?

What does faithfulness look like for you when suffering or storms seem to endure?

Prayer

God our Creator, you do not abandon us even when we mess up the world you have made. Help us to attend to your call, that we may faithfully respond and be part of the healing and restoration of your world. *Amen.*

Genesis 8

8 But God remembered Noah and all the wild animals and all the domestic animals that were with him in the ark. And God made a wind blow over the earth, and the waters subsided; ²the fountains of the deep and the windows of the heavens were closed, the rain from the heavens was restrained, ³and the waters gradually receded from the earth. At the end of one hundred fifty days the waters had abated;

⁴and in the seventh month, on the seventeenth day of the month, the ark came to rest on the mountains of Ararat. ⁵The waters continued to abate until the tenth month; in the tenth month, on the first day of the month, the tops of the mountains appeared.

⁶At the end of forty days Noah opened the window of the ark that he had made ⁷and sent out the raven; and it went to and fro until the waters were dried up from the earth. ⁸Then he sent out the dove from him, to see if the waters had subsided from the face of the ground; ⁹but the dove found no place to set its foot, and it returned to him to the ark, for the waters were still on the face of the whole earth. So he put out his hand and took it and brought it into the ark with him. ¹⁰He waited another seven days, and again he sent out the dove from the ark; ¹¹and the dove came back to him in the evening, and there in its beak was a freshly plucked olive leaf; so Noah knew that the waters had subsided from the earth. ¹²Then he waited another seven days, and sent out the dove; and it did not return to him any more.

¹³In the six hundred first year, in the first month, the first day of the month, the waters were dried up from the earth; and Noah removed the covering of the ark, and looked, and saw that the face of the ground was drying. ¹⁴In the second month, on the twenty-seventh day of the month, the earth was dry.

¹⁵Then God said to Noah, ¹⁶"Go out of the ark, you and your wife, and your sons and your sons' wives with you. ¹⁷Bring out with you every living thing that is with you of all flesh—birds and animals and every creeping thing that creeps on the earth—so that they may abound on the earth, and be fruitful and multiply on the earth." ¹⁸So Noah went out with his sons and his wife and his sons' wives. ¹⁹And every animal, every creeping thing, and every bird, everything that moves on the earth, went out of the ark by families.

²⁰Then Noah built an altar to the Lord, and took of every clean animal and of every clean bird, and offered burnt offerings on the altar. ²¹And when the Lord smelled the pleasing odor, the Lord said in his heart, "I will never again curse the ground because of humankind, for the inclination of the human heart is evil from youth; nor will I ever again destroy every living creature as I have done. ²²As long as the earth endures, seedtime and harvest, cold and heat, summer and winter, day and night, shall not cease."

Reflection

Even after what may seem like interminable storms in our lives, God's promises reveal new life and hope. The waters of the flood recede gradually, and Noah's family and the animals of the ark are able to escape their long nautical confinement. God calls them to be fruitful and multiply, echoing humanity's original call in the Garden of Eden. A new beginning is possible.

Notice that humanity hasn't really changed in this story; God makes clear that the inclination of the human heart tends toward evil. People will still mess up and do violence to one another and to God's creation. Human nature is broken at a deep level.

It is God who changes. God chooses not to destroy the world again unconditionally: not *if* humans do better, but regardless. God makes a promise that does not depend on humans getting things right or living up to our end of the bargain. God knows we will always struggle to do so.

This idea of God's unconditional promise is so powerful and revolutionary that many people do not really believe it. They think God's love for them is contingent upon not making mistakes, not doing wrong, and never messing up. But this story does not say humans will never again mess up. We will hurt one another and turn our backs on God. Yet, God's love is bigger and embraces us regardless. This is most poignantly embodied on the cross, where Jesus suffers unjust torture and violence and still offers forgiveness to those who put him there.

God's love is not up to you! Is that not great news? And if so, then we can stop worrying about where we stand before God and focus instead on loving our neighbors. We can, like Noah, lift our hearts in worship of our Creator, and then be fruitful and bless the earth.

— **The Rev. Dr. Dwight Zscheile**

Questions

Have you ever felt like God's love was dependent on you getting everything right?

What might it look like for you to live in the freedom and security of God's unconditional love? How might that change how you treat your neighbors and God's creation?

Prayer

God of mercy, you bring healing and new life even amidst suffering and distress. You know we are not perfect and often choose wrongly. Help us to sink into the arms of your steadfast love so that we might lead lives of worship, praise, freedom, and service. *Amen.*

Genesis 9

9 God blessed Noah and his sons, and said to them, "Be fruitful and multiply, and fill the earth. ²The fear and dread of you shall rest on every animal of the earth, and on every bird of the air, on everything that creeps on the ground, and on all the fish of the sea; into your hand they are delivered. ³Every moving thing that lives shall be food for you; and just as I gave you the green plants, I give you everything. ⁴Only, you shall not eat flesh with its life, that is, its blood. ⁵For your own lifeblood I will surely require a reckoning: from every animal I will require it and from human beings, each one for the blood of another, I will require a reckoning for human life. ⁶Whoever sheds the blood of a human, by a human shall that person's blood be shed; for in his own image God made humankind. ⁷And you, be fruitful and multiply, abound on the earth and multiply in it."

⁸Then God said to Noah and to his sons with him, ⁹"As for me, I am establishing my covenant with you and your descendants after you, ¹⁰and with every living creature that is with you, the birds, the domestic animals, and every animal of the earth with you, as many as came out of the ark. ¹¹I establish my covenant with you, that never again shall all flesh be cut off by the waters of a flood, and never again shall there be a flood to destroy the earth."

¹²God said, "This is the sign of the covenant that I make between me and you and every living creature that is with you, for all future generations: ¹³I have set my bow in the clouds, and it shall be a sign of the covenant between me and the earth.

¹⁴When I bring clouds over the earth and the bow is seen in the clouds, ¹⁵I will remember my covenant that is between me and you and every living creature of all flesh; and the waters shall never again become a flood to destroy all flesh. ¹⁶When the bow is in the clouds, I will see it and remember the everlasting covenant between God and every living creature of all flesh that is on the earth." ¹⁷God said to Noah, "This is the sign of the covenant that I have established between me and all flesh that is on the earth."

¹⁸The sons of Noah who went out of the ark were Shem, Ham, and Japheth. Ham was the father of Canaan. ¹⁹These three were the sons of Noah; and from these the whole earth was peopled. ²⁰Noah, a man of the soil, was the first to plant a vineyard. ²¹He drank some of the wine and became drunk, and he lay uncovered in his tent. ²²And Ham, the father of Canaan, saw the nakedness of his father, and told his two brothers outside. ²³Then Shem and Japheth took a garment, laid it on both their shoulders, and walked backward and covered the nakedness of their father; their faces were turned away, and they did not see their father's nakedness.

²⁴When Noah awoke from his wine and knew what his youngest son had done to him, ²⁵he said, "Cursed be Canaan; lowest of slaves shall he be to his brothers." ²⁶He also said, "Blessed by the LORD my God be Shem; and let Canaan be his slave. ²⁷May God make space for Japheth, and let him live in the tents of Shem; and let Canaan be his slave."

²⁸After the flood Noah lived three hundred fifty years. ²⁹All the days of Noah were nine hundred fifty years; and he died.

Reflection

"God blessed Noah and his sons, and said to them, 'Be fruitful and multiply...'" The ninth chapter of Genesis begins with these familiar words. God blesses Noah and his sons and tells them what to do now that the flood has passed. Go out into the world and begin again. Biblical scholars refer to this as the "fertility blessing."

Next, God initiates a new covenant between Noah and his family. "I establish my covenant with you, that never again shall all flesh be cut off by the waters of a flood..." The New Oxford Annotated Bible tells us that "this is the first covenant explicitly described as such in the Bible." And what is a sign for us, even today, of this covenant? The rainbow.

In *The Torah: A Women's Commentary,* Rabbi Tamara Cohn Eskenazi tells us that "the transgressions that led to the flood transform God's expectations. They result in new rules to guide humankind and a promise of a perpetual covenant. God's blessings and God's new instructions signal a new beginning."

The Christian concept of reconciliation means that we are restored again in our relationship, our union with God. There can also be reconciliation between two or more people, especially in families. God is always calling us home. We have been invited to a new beginning with God, to draw closer to him.

You may have not spent a year on the ark like Noah but perhaps you have drifted about in a storm-tossed sea of doubt, anger, frustration, loneliness, or fear. Take comfort in the message of this chapter as you seek to draw closer to your creator.

As Rabbi Eskenazi writes, "The covenant emphasizes renewal. It also offers the assurance of security to humankind. The covenant reiterates the perpetuity of its promise and its expansive scope, encompassing all living beings." God's covenant is as relevant now as it was in the time of Noah. God wants to be in relationship with you and his promise is as fresh today as it was when the first rainbow appeared in the sky.

— Lynne Jordal Martin

Questions

What kind of a relationship with God do you have?

What kind of a relationship would you like to have? If it's time for a new beginning, ask God to show you what it would look like and to guide you to it.

Is there someone who needs your forgiveness, with whom would you like to start over again?

Prayer

Lord, you have searched me and known me. You have a vision of a new beginning for me in my relationship with you. Show me the life you have in mind for me. And show me those with whom I need to be reconciled today. *Amen.*

A Journey through Genesis

Genesis 10

10 These are the descendants of Noah's sons, Shem, Ham, and Japheth; children were born to them after the flood. ²The descendants of Japheth: Gomer, Magog, Madai, Javan, Tubal, Meshech, and Tiras. ³The descendants of Gomer: Ashkenaz, Riphath, and Togarmah. ⁴The descendants of Javan: Elishah, Tarshish, Kittim, and Rodanim. ⁵From these the coastland peoples spread. These are the descendants of Japheth in their lands, with their own language, by their families, in their nations.

⁶The descendants of Ham: Cush, Egypt, Put, and Canaan. ⁷The descendants of Cush: Seba, Havilah, Sabtah, Raamah, and Sabteca. The descendants of Raamah: Sheba and Dedan. ⁸Cush became the father of Nimrod; he was the first on earth to become a mighty warrior. ⁹He was a mighty hunter before the LORD; therefore it is said, "Like Nimrod a mighty hunter before the LORD." ¹⁰The beginning of his kingdom was Babel, Erech, and Accad, all of them in the land of Shinar. ¹¹From that land he went into Assyria, and built Nineveh, Rehoboth-ir, Calah, and ¹²Resen between Nineveh and Calah; that is the great city. ¹³Egypt became the father of Ludim, Anamim, Lehabim, Naphtuhim, ¹⁴Pathrusim, Casluhim, and Caphtorim, from which the Philistines come.

¹⁵Canaan became the father of Sidon his firstborn, and Heth, ¹⁶and the Jebusites, the Amorites, the Girgashites, ¹⁷the Hivites, the Arkites, the Sinites, ¹⁸the Arvadites, the Zemarites, and the Hamathites. Afterward the families of the Canaanites

spread abroad. ¹⁹And the territory of the Canaanites extended from Sidon, in the direction of Gerar, as far as Gaza, and in the direction of Sodom, Gomorrah, Admah, and Zeboiim, as far as Lasha. ²⁰These are the descendants of Ham, by their families, their languages, their lands, and their nations.

²¹To Shem also, the father of all the children of Eber, the elder brother of Japheth, children were born. ²²The descendants of Shem: Elam, Asshur, Arpachshad, Lud, and Aram. ²³The descendants of Aram: Uz, Hul, Gether, and Mash. ²⁴Arpachshad became the father of Shelah; and Shelah became the father of Eber. ²⁵To Eber were born two sons: the name of the one was Peleg, for in his days the earth was divided, and his brother's name was Joktan. ²⁶Joktan became the father of Almodad, Sheleph, Hazarmaveth, Jerah, ²⁷Hadoram, Uzal, Diklah, ²⁸Obal, Abimael, Sheba, ²⁹Ophir, Havilah, and Jobab; all these were the descendants of Joktan. ³⁰The territory in which they lived extended from Mesha in the direction of Sephar, the hill country of the east. ³¹These are the descendants of Shem, by their families, their languages, their lands, and their nations. ³²These are the families of Noah's sons, according to their genealogies, in their nations; and from these the nations spread abroad on the earth after the flood.

Reflection

This chapter is often referred to as the Table of Nations. It's the story of how Noah's sons and their families spread out over many lands after the flood. The New Oxford Annotated Bible tells us that this chapter is "a (largely Priestly) survey of the world of the Israelites. Like many ancient peoples, they depicted the relations between national groups in kinship terms." At the end of the chapter we read, "these are the families of Noah's sons, according to their genealogies, in their nations, and from these the nations spread abroad on earth after the flood."

In the previous chapter, the fertility blessing was reaffirmed. Noah's sons were told to be fruitful and multiply. So, what does this all mean for you and me? Earlier in Genesis we are clearly told that human beings have been created in God's own image. God created you and me and adopted us as his children.

What is our spiritual inheritance as children of God? We are loved just as Noah and his sons and their families were. Each of us is unique and precious. In the Holy Eucharist Rite II, we hear these words, "Holy and gracious Father: In your infinite love you made us for yourself." We were made for God. God's infinite love created you and me. We are descendants of Noah; we are inheritors of the promise God made after the flood.

What have we inherited? A fresh start. The Rev. Scott Gunn, executive director of Forward Movement, has written that Christianity is a religion of second chances. "It starts in the Old Testament," he writes, "where God sends prophets again and again to remind his people how to live. And over and over, the people reject the prophets. Still, God never gives up on his people. He continues to invite people to a more loving way of living."

God also asks us to offer others second chances through forgiveness and grace. May we be fruitful in the love of God and multiply it today and every day for the rest of our lives.

— **Lynne Jordal Martin**

Questions_____

What spiritual teachings and insights have you inherited from your family and community of faith?

What are some of the spiritual gifts you have received from God?

Prayer _____

Beloved creator, you have made me in your image. Help me to see your reflection clearly in my life and works. Let me rejoice in the life I have inherited as your child. Show me how to invite others into the life of faith I have been given by you. *Amen.*

Genesis 11

11 Now the whole earth had one language and the same words. ²And as they migrated from the east, they came upon a plain in the land of Shinar and settled there. ³And they said to one another, "Come, let us make bricks, and burn them thoroughly." And they had brick for stone, and bitumen for mortar. ⁴Then they said, "Come, let us build ourselves a city, and a tower with its top in the heavens, and let us make a name for ourselves; otherwise we shall be scattered abroad upon the face of the whole earth."

⁵The LORD came down to see the city and the tower, which mortals had built. ⁶And the LORD said, "Look, they are one people, and they have all one language; and this is only the beginning of what they will do; nothing that they propose to do will now be impossible for them. ⁷Come, let us go down, and confuse their language there, so that they will not understand one another's speech." ⁸So the LORD scattered them abroad from there over the face of all the earth, and they left off building the city. ⁹Therefore it was called Babel, because there the LORD confused the language of all the earth; and from there the LORD scattered them abroad over the face of all the earth.

¹⁰These are the descendants of Shem. When Shem was one hundred years old, he became the father of Arpachshad two years after the flood; ¹¹and Shem lived after the birth of Arpachshad five hundred years, and had other sons and daughters. ¹²When Arpachshad had lived thirty-five years, he

became the father of Shelah; [13]and Arpachshad lived after the birth of Shelah four hundred three years, and had other sons and daughters. [14]When Shelah had lived thirty years, he became the father of Eber; [15]and Shelah lived after the birth of Eber four hundred three years, and had other sons and daughters. [16]When Eber had lived thirty-four years, he became the father of Peleg; [17]and Eber lived after the birth of Peleg four hundred thirty years, and had other sons and daughters. [18]When Peleg had lived thirty years, he became the father of Reu; [19]and Peleg lived after the birth of Reu two hundred nine years, and had other sons and daughters. [20]When Reu had lived thirty-two years, he became the father of Serug; [21]and Reu lived after the birth of Serug two hundred seven years, and had other sons and daughters. [22]When Serug had lived thirty years, he became the father of Nahor; [23]and Serug lived after the birth of Nahor two hundred years, and had other sons and daughters. [24]When Nahor had lived twenty-nine years, he became the father of Terah; [25]and Nahor lived after the birth of Terah one hundred nineteen years, and had other sons and daughters. [26]When Terah had lived seventy years, he became the father of Abram, Nahor, and Haran.

[27]Now these are the descendants of Terah. Terah was the father of Abram, Nahor, and Haran; and Haran was the father of Lot. [28]Haran died before his father Terah in the land of his birth, in Ur of the Chaldeans. [29]Abram and Nahor took wives; the name of Abram's wife was Sarai, and the name of Nahor's wife was Milcah. She was the daughter of Haran the father of Milcah and Iscah. [30]Now Sarai was barren; she had no child. [31]Terah took his son Abram and his grandson Lot son of Haran,

and his daughter-in-law Sarai, his son Abram's wife, and they went out together from Ur of the Chaldeans to go into the land of Canaan; but when they came to Haran, they settled there. [32]The days of Terah were two hundred five years; and Terah died in Haran.

Reflection

The Tower of Babel is one of the Bible's greatest stories. It is an extrapolation of Adam and Eve's expulsion in the Garden of Eden where the "first disobedience" occurred, leading to their dispersal and journey east, where Cain was eventually condemned to wander after killing his brother (Genesis 4:16).

This story of the Tower of Babel is rooted in ancient Sumerian, Mesopotamian, and Babylonian civilizations. It seeks to explain why there is such a great diversity of languages in the world, which create barriers among people. Similar tales are told in other ancient cultures. Genesis notes that the inhabitants baked bricks and used bitumen for mortar to build the tower, but these were not Palestinian building materials. Hence, the story may have originated elsewhere.

The tower may well have been a ziggurat, one of those huge, sacred Mesopotamia towers that were square or rectangular structures with each ascending level shorter than the previous one and having staircases and ramps to allow persons to ascend and descend. At the top was a shrine. The purpose of the ziggurat was to allow the gods to descend to earth.

The author of the story of the Tower of Babel turns the ziggurat on its head. This tower is now a means to ascend to God. The idea of a conduit between heaven and earth is mirrored later in Genesis. When Jacob wakes from his dream, he says, "How awesome is this place! This is none other than the house of God [*Beth-el* in Hebrew] and this is the gate of heaven" (Genesis 28:17).

The building of the tower is seen as an example of human sin and pride. We cut ourselves off from God when we think too highly or frequently of ourselves and assume that we have godlike powers and no limitations. We often do not know when and where to halt using our powers and to recognize that we are part of God's world.

This over-trusting in ourselves and disconnection from God comes with a price. We create divisions, rupturing relationships, and in the grander scheme, these actions pit nations, races, religions, social classes, and political parties against each other. We become tribal, with each group having its own language and customs, no longer able to effectively communicate with and trust others. God's vision of Eden is transformed by our hubris into a dispersal like Babel.

Yet, there is another way of viewing this story. In his book *The Dignity of Difference*, Rabbi Jonathan Sachs refers to the story of Babel as the "first totalitarianism." Totalitarianism is where we must think one thought, speak one language, have one religion, and follow one political party. In lectures and in books, Sachs suggests that the great diversity of humanity is actually one of God's finest blessings and not a curse. That's a message for us today.

— The Rev. Marek P. Zabriskie

Questions _____

Where do you see the story of the Tower of Babel being enacted out in the world today?

Where in your life do you worry that harmony is being sacrificed to prideful aspirations?

Do you see diversity and different languages, customs, races, religions, practices, political parties, social classes, and nations as a threat or as something that enriches our world?

Prayer _____

O Gracious God, you are the architect of our universe. Be patient with us, your children, who often fancy ourselves as brighter, more capable, more intelligent, more worthy, and more independent than we should. We do not know how to stop being masters of our own existence. Help us to bind ourselves closer to you so that we might live in greater harmony with each other. *Amen.*

Genesis 12

12 Now the LORD said to Abram, "Go from your country and your kindred and your father's house to the land that I will show you. ²I will make of you a great nation, and I will bless you, and make your name great, so that you will be a blessing. ³I will bless those who bless you, and the one who curses you I will curse; and in you all the families of the earth shall be blessed."

⁴So Abram went, as the LORD had told him; and Lot went with him. Abram was seventy-five years old when he departed from Haran. ⁵Abram took his wife Sarai and his brother's son Lot, and all the possessions that they had gathered, and the persons whom they had acquired in Haran; and they set forth to go to the land of Canaan. When they had come to the land of Canaan,

⁶Abram passed through the land to the place at Shechem, to the oak of Moreh. At that time the Canaanites were in the land. ⁷Then the LORD appeared to Abram, and said, "To your offspring I will give this land." So he built there an altar to the LORD, who had appeared to him. ⁸From there he moved on to the hill country on the east of Bethel, and pitched his tent, with Bethel on the west and Ai on the east; and there he built an altar to the LORD and invoked the name of the LORD. ⁹And Abram journeyed on by stages toward the Negeb.

¹⁰Now there was a famine in the land. So Abram went down to Egypt to reside there as an alien, for the famine was severe in the

land. [11]When he was about to enter Egypt, he said to his wife Sarai, "I know well that you are a woman beautiful in appearance; [12]and when the Egyptians see you, they will say, 'This is his wife'; then they will kill me, but they will let you live. [13]Say you are my sister, so that it may go well with me because of you, and that my life may be spared on your account."

[14]When Abram entered Egypt the Egyptians saw that the woman was very beautiful. [15]When the officials of Pharaoh saw her, they praised her to Pharaoh. And the woman was taken into Pharaoh's house. [16]And for her sake he dealt well with Abram; and he had sheep, oxen, male donkeys, male and female slaves, female donkeys, and camels. [17]But the LORD afflicted Pharaoh and his house with great plagues because of Sarai, Abram's wife. [18]So Pharaoh called Abram, and said, "What is this you have done to me? Why did you not tell me that she was your wife? [19]Why did you say, 'She is my sister,' so that I took her for my wife? Now then, here is your wife, take her, and be gone." [20]And Pharaoh gave his men orders concerning him; and they set him on the way, with his wife and all that he had.

Reflection

The book of Genesis includes two main parts: chapters 1-11 and 12-50. The first section focuses on primeval history—the history of the cosmos and the first humans. The second part focuses on ancestral history, namely Abraham and Sarah and their descendants. This chapter is thus the beginning of the second part.

Chapter 12 offers us the call of Abraham. It is one of the great call narratives of the Bible. These are stories where God intervenes in someone's life and invites a person to take on a special role. Call narratives have commonalities. The person called is often surprised. Their first reaction is often to run in the opposite direction or oppose God's call by noting that they are unsuited or ill-equipped to accept God's assignment. Moses, for example, tells God that he has no ability to speak in public (Exodus 4:10-16). God persists.

God offers a promise in each call narrative. "If you do this, I, Yahweh, will bless you." But there is always a cost to bear. The call recipient must be willing to make sacrifices in order to serve God. The call of Abraham is classic. It is the first of three divine speeches in which a patriarch is given travel directions and promises of blessing (Genesis 12:1-3; 26:2-5; 46:1-4).

God instructs Abraham (who is known at the time as "Abram") to "Go from your country and your kindred and your father's house to the land that I will show you" (Genesis 12:1). Hence, Abraham and Sarah must leave family and all that is familiar to them to follow God's call. But herein lies the promise. God says, "I will make of you a great nation, and I will bless you, and make your name great, so that you will be a blessing."

The promise of a great nation stands in tension with Abraham's barren wife, Sarah. This tension will play out until chapter 21 when the aged Sarah gives birth. The idea of nation implies not just many people but a new, independent social entity. "I will bless you" and "make your name great" implies wealth and becoming famous. For a moment, this sounds like the prosperity gospel, where proponents claim that God wants to make us rich and successful.

One of the surprises of Genesis is how many characters appear more like rogues than saints. Abraham is no exception. He puts his wife in jeopardy to protect himself, passing her off as his sister to spare his own life. She is taken into Pharoah's concubine (Genesis 12) and King Abimelech's household (Genesis 20). Only a plague afflicting Pharoah's household and a dream warning Abimelech spare Sarah from harm.

While Abraham is known as "faithful," he often comes across as faithless. His descendants like Jacob are masters of trickery. We are left wondering what to make of these cagey characters. Clearly, God carves the rotten wood and uses fallen human beings to carry out divine means. Perhaps there's hope for us.

— **The Rev. Marek P. Zabriskie**

Questions _____

Are you ever troubled by the moral nature of biblical figures, wondering how God can use such flawed persons to carry out God's will? Who comes to mind?

Have you ever heard or sensed God call your name and invite you into a new role or to take on a specific charge? Did you heed God's call or run in the opposite direction or offer excuses as to why you were not equipped or capable or worthy to accept God's call?

What is God inviting you to do right now in your life? Have you asked some close family members or friends to help you discern what you sense you are being led to do? Have you taken it to prayer and asked God to clarify what you should do and to inspire you to do it?

Prayer _____

Merciful God, we are the rotten wood that you carve and the flawed children that you call into service. We long to serve you but feel ourselves to be unworthy of carrying out your will. Help us not to play small and to erect barricades of excuses. Give us the courage to make sacrifices so that we may accept the roles you invite us to shoulder, trusting you will bless and equip us to carry out your charge. *Amen.*

Genesis 13

13 So Abram went up from Egypt, he and his wife, and all that he had, and Lot with him, into the Negeb. ²Now Abram was very rich in livestock, in silver, and in gold. ³He journeyed on by stages from the Negeb as far as Bethel, to the place where his tent had been at the beginning, between Bethel and Ai, ⁴to the place where he had made an altar at the first; and there Abram called on the name of the LORD.

⁵Now Lot, who went with Abram, also had flocks and herds and tents, ⁶so that the land could not support both of them living together; for their possessions were so great that they could not live together, ⁷and there was strife between the herders of Abram's livestock and the herders of Lot's livestock. At that time the Canaanites

and the Perizzites lived in the land. ⁸Then Abram said to Lot, "Let there be no strife between you and me, and between your herders and my herders; for we are kindred. ⁹Is not the whole land before you? Separate yourself from me. If you take the left hand, then I will go to the right; or if you take the right hand, then I will go to the left."

¹⁰Lot looked about him, and saw that the plain of the Jordan was well watered everywhere like the garden of the LORD, like the land of Egypt, in the direction of Zoar; this was before the LORD had destroyed Sodom and Gomorrah. ¹¹So Lot chose for himself all the plain of the Jordan, and Lot journeyed eastward; thus they separated from each other. ¹²Abram settled in the land of Canaan, while Lot settled among the

cities of the Plain and moved his tent as far as Sodom. ¹³Now the people of Sodom were wicked, great sinners against the LORD.

¹⁴The LORD said to Abram, after Lot had separated from him, "Raise your eyes now, and look from the place where you are, northward and southward and eastward and westward; ¹⁵for all the land that you see I will give to you and to your offspring forever. ¹⁶I will make your offspring like the dust of the earth; so that if one can count the dust of the earth, your offspring also can be counted. ¹⁷Rise up, walk through the length and the breadth of the land, for I will give it to you." ¹⁸So Abram moved his tent, and came and settled by the oaks of Mamre, which are at Hebron; and there he built an altar to the LORD.

Reflection

Every family has ups and downs—even "in the beginning." In this chapter of Genesis, we can appreciate how Abram and his nephew Lot felt forced to part ways due to a variety of circumstances. Whether one is a member of the British royal family or part of an average family anywhere on God's planet, we can all agree that family unity is an ideal that most of us struggle with throughout life—and it was no different for Abram and Lot, even way back then.

One of the greatest pastoral challenges I have often encountered in my 30 years as an ordained minister in the church has been to witness families suffer pains and consequences of separation at some point in their lives. Sometimes, this strife is motivated by material possessions, for instance, after the reading of a will. Other times, the suffering stems from the result of a broken marriage and the painful consequences of separation and divorce. In some cases, families pull apart because of different worldviews or values.

In the specific case of Abram and Lot, it appears that going their separate ways was a measure taken out of respect to one another: the motivation appears to be a positive one to avoid strife between family members. Perhaps Genesis 13 contains a practical lesson for believers of our times: at times, keeping a healthy distance can help preserve long-term relationships.

In Spanish, we have a popular saying, *"Juntos, pero no revueltos,"* which literally translated means, "Together but not scrambled." In other words, we can be together and love each other without having to be so close all the time. Healthy boundaries can go a long way. Abram and Lot create some space and physical separation with the desire of avoiding strife in their family—yet neither of them is aware of the challenges to come.

— The Rev. Alberto R. Cutié

Questions

After reading and reflecting on Genesis 13, what lessons are there in the separation of Abram and Lot?

Have there been times in your life when you have felt the pain of a family separation? How did those circumstances impact your life?

Abram and Lot, although influenced by their workers who are unhappy, make peace with each other. Is there a time when boundaries, in your own family life or that of others, have been difficult to make?

Prayer

God of peace, help us to know the importance of healthy boundaries, even with those we love so closely. May the example of Abram and Lot motivate us to respect each other, despite the many differences that may arise in all our human relationships. Make us ever more aware of the gifts of our individuality and our diversity. *Amen*.

Genesis 14

14 In the days of King Amraphel of Shinar, King Arioch of Ellasar, King Chedorlaomer of Elam, and King Tidal of Goiim, ²these kings made war with King Bera of Sodom, King Birsha of Gomorrah, King Shinab of Admah, King Shemeber of Zeboiim, and the king of Bela (that is, Zoar). ³All these joined forces in the Valley of Siddim (that is, the Dead Sea). ⁴Twelve years they had served Chedorlaomer, but in the thirteenth year they rebelled. ⁵In the fourteenth year Chedorlaomer and the kings who were with him came and subdued the Rephaim in Ashteroth-karnaim, the Zuzim in Ham, the Emim in Shaveh-kiriathaim, ⁶and the Horites in the hill country of Seir as far as El-paran on the edge of the wilderness; ⁷then they turned back and came to En-mishpat (that is, Kadesh), and subdued all the country of the Amalekites, and also the Amorites who lived in Hazazon-tamar. ⁸Then the king of Sodom, the king of Gomorrah, the king of Admah, the king of Zeboiim, and the king of Bela (that is, Zoar) went out, and they joined battle in the Valley of Siddim ⁹with King Chedorlaomer of Elam, King Tidal of Goiim, King Amraphel of Shinar, and King Arioch of Ellasar, four kings against five. ¹⁰Now the Valley of Siddim was full of bitumen pits; and as the kings of Sodom and Gomorrah fled, some fell into them, and the rest fled to the hill country. ¹¹So the enemy took all the goods of Sodom and Gomorrah, and all their provisions, and went their way; ¹²they also took Lot,

the son of Abram's brother, who lived in Sodom, and his goods, and departed.

13Then one who had escaped came and told Abram the Hebrew, who was living by the oaks of Mamre the Amorite, brother of Eshcol and of Aner; these were allies of Abram. 14When Abram heard that his nephew had been taken captive, he led forth his trained men, born in his house, three hundred eighteen of them, and went in pursuit as far as Dan. 15He divided his forces against them by night, he and his servants, and routed them and pursued them to Hobah, north of Damascus. 16Then he brought back all the goods, and also brought back his nephew Lot with his goods, and the women and the people.

17After his return from the defeat of Chedorlaomer and the kings who were with him, the king of Sodom went out to meet him at the Valley of Shaveh (that is, the King's Valley). 18And King Melchizedek of Salem brought out bread and wine; he was priest of God Most High. 19He blessed him and said, "Blessed be Abram by God Most High, maker of heaven and earth; 20and blessed be God Most High, who has delivered your enemies into your hand!" And Abram gave him one tenth of everything.

21Then the king of Sodom said to Abram, "Give me the persons, but take the goods for yourself." 22But Abram said to the king of Sodom, "I have sworn to the LORD, God Most High, maker of heaven and earth, 23that I would not take a thread or a sandal-thong or anything that is yours, so that you might not say, 'I have made Abram rich.' 24I will take nothing but what the young men have eaten, and the share of the men who went with me—Aner, Eshcol, and Mamre. Let them take their share."

Reflection

As we read and reflect on Genesis 14, we are immediately presented with a list of kings with long names who are all at war with each other. Some rebel against the authorities they have served for years, and this leads to multiple battles. Lot, the nephew of Abram, is among those attacked and sacked. Luckily for Lot, Abram deploys 318 of his trained men to rescue him and his property. The separation between Abram and Lot does not keep Abram from being a generous and caring uncle.

In this chapter, I am instantly struck by the generosity of Abram. He does not hesitate to reach out in care for Lot and to use all his resources to rescue him and to recover what was stolen from him. When Abram returns from his mission, he pays a tithe—an offering of 10% of all that was recovered—to Melchizedek, King and High Priest of Salem (later known as Jerusalem). Abram's offering is one of those places in sacred scripture where we find a clear biblical and practical custom of tithing.

Melchizedek recognizes the generosity and faithfulness of Abram. It is precisely here, in Genesis 14, that we find a very significant blessing upon Abram with the offering of bread and wine made by Melchizedek as both the king and priest of Salem. For this reason, many scripture scholars will refer to Melchizedek as a "type of Christ," making references to the eucharistic banquet that Jesus establishes in the new and everlasting covenant.

— **The Rev. Alberto R. Cutié**

Questions

What impact does the response of Abram to Lot's captivity have on you as a reader and person of faith?

What lessons can we take away from the generosity of Abram and the practice of tithing?

What connections do you perceive in the offering of bread and wine by Melchizedek and the offering of Jesus in the eucharist?

Prayer

God of generous love, may the example of Abram, who went out of his way to help his relative in need with all of his resources, motivate us to never grow indifferent toward the call of those who suffer and need our help. May we be generous with our time, our talents, and our treasure, as we seek to build up your kingdom of love in our world and in our present time. *Amen.*

Genesis 15

15 After these things the word of the LORD came to Abram in a vision, "Do not be afraid, Abram, I am your shield; your reward shall be very great."

²But Abram said, "O LORD God, what will you give me, for I continue childless, and the heir of my house is Eliezer of Damascus?" ³And Abram said, "You have given me no offspring, and so a slave born in my house is to be my heir." ⁴But the word of the LORD came to him, "This man shall not be your heir; no one but your very own issue shall be your heir." ⁵He brought him outside and said, "Look toward heaven and count the stars, if you are able to count them." Then he said to him, "So shall your descendants be." ⁶And he believed the LORD; and the LORD reckoned it to him as righteousness.

⁷Then he said to him, "I am the LORD who brought you from Ur of the Chaldeans, to give you this land to possess." ⁸But he said, "O LORD God, how am I to know that I shall possess it?" ⁹He said to him, "Bring me a heifer three years old, a female goat three years old, a ram three years old, a turtledove, and a young pigeon." ¹⁰He brought him all these and cut them in two, laying each half over against the other; but he did not cut the birds in two. ¹¹And when birds of prey came down on the carcasses, Abram drove them away.

¹²As the sun was going down, a deep sleep fell upon Abram, and a deep and terrifying darkness descended upon him. ¹³Then the LORD said to Abram, "Know this for certain, that your offspring shall be aliens in a

land that is not theirs, and shall be slaves there, and they shall be oppressed for four hundred years; [14]but I will bring judgment on the nation that they serve, and afterward they shall come out with great possessions. [15]As for yourself, you shall go to your ancestors in peace; you shall be buried in a good old age. [16]And they shall come back here in the fourth generation; for the iniquity of the Amorites is not yet complete."

[17]When the sun had gone down and it was dark, a smoking fire pot and a flaming torch passed between these pieces. [18]On that day the LORD made a covenant with Abram, saying, "To your descendants I give this land, from the river of Egypt to the great river, the river Euphrates, [19]the land of the Kenites, the Kenizzites, the Kadmonites, [20]the Hittites, the Perizzites, the Rephaim, [21]the Amorites, the Canaanites, the Girgashites, and the Jebusites."

Reflection

Among the many things that separate us from the world of Genesis is the readiness with which the divine reveals itself to the human. The word of the Lord comes to Abram and Hagar four times in these two chapters, directly in a vison to Abram (Genesis 15) and indirectly through the mediation of an angel to Hagar (Genesis 16). We find an open channel of communication between heaven and earth, not quite as close as when God "walked" with Adam and Eve "in the garden at the time of the evening breeze" (Genesis 3:8), when contact seems to have been every day, but still far closer than many of us would experience today.

God is especially attentive to the anxieties of his chosen humans, understanding what makes them confused and afraid, and intervening with information to allay fears. Sometimes the contact is spectacular as when God addresses Abram's concerns about the future in a "deep and terrifying darkness" (Genesis 15:12), wherein a covenant is made. Sometimes it transpires quietly in an angel's conversation, as when a messenger of the Lord comforts the enslaved Hagar, not only with promises of future for her son but also with the staggering experience of divine presence: "Have I really seen God and remained alive, after seeing him?" (Genesis 16:13).

But if Abram, Sarai, and Hagar are caught up in a drama of divine intimacy foreign to most of us, the concerns that drive them to God are as common to us as daily bread. Abram has no heir to carry on his line or to fulfill the divine expectation of a progeny as countless as the stars. What will he do? Sarai is barren and in domestic warfare with a pregnant Hagar, who Sarai herself chose to bear an heir to

Abram. To flee Sarai's wrath, Hagar takes flight with her newborn son, a refugee escaping to a wilderness where surely death awaits.

In the midst of this recognizably messy human tangle, God is mysteriously working out a divine promise for the future. Abram will have descendants—and not only with the fertile Hagar but also with the barren Sarai. His nomadic people will dwell in their own land stretching from the Nile to the Euphrates (Genesis 15:18). His progeny may not see God and live as vividly he did, but they will survive. Life, indeed, will have the last word.

— Dr. Peter S. Hawkins

Questions

In what ways have you felt yourself part of a divine plan?

You have probably not had a vision like Abram or conversed with an angel like Hagar. Nonetheless, how has God "spoken" to you?

Note how Genesis presents a chosen people "warts and all," without idealization. Does this ring true to you?

Prayer

O God, your ways are not our ways, nor do we hear or see you as our ancestors in faith did. Even so, help us to have our ears and eyes open to you. Give us the patience to wait on you for understanding and the perseverance to hold on to you when fear would have us let go. Keep us attentive in the wilderness. *Amen.*

Genesis 16

16 Now Sarai, Abram's wife, bore him no children. She had an Egyptian slave-girl whose name was Hagar, ²and Sarai said to Abram, "You see that the LORD has prevented me from bearing children; go in to my slave-girl; it may be that I shall obtain children by her." And Abram listened to the voice of Sarai. ³So, after Abram had lived ten years in the land of Canaan, Sarai, Abram's wife, took Hagar the Egyptian, her slave-girl, and gave her to her husband Abram as a wife.

⁴He went in to Hagar, and she conceived; and when she saw that she had conceived, she looked with contempt on her mistress. ⁵Then Sarai said to Abram, "May the wrong done to me be on you! I gave my slave-girl to your embrace, and when she saw that she had conceived, she looked on me with contempt. May the LORD judge between you and me!" ⁶But Abram said to Sarai, "Your slave-girl is in your power; do to her as you please." Then Sarai dealt harshly with her, and she ran away from her.

⁷The angel of the LORD found her by a spring of water in the wilderness, the spring on the way to Shur. ⁸And he said, "Hagar, slave-girl of Sarai, where have you come from and where are you going?" She said, "I am running away from my mistress Sarai." ⁹The angel of the LORD said to her, "Return to your mistress, and submit to her."

¹⁰The angel of the LORD also said to her, "I will so greatly

multiply your offspring that they cannot be counted for multitude." [11]And the angel of the LORD said to her, "Now you have conceived and shall bear a son; you shall call him Ishmael, for the LORD has given heed to your affliction. [12]He shall be a wild ass of a man, with his hand against everyone, and everyone's hand against him; and he shall live at odds with all his kin."

[13]So she named the LORD who spoke to her, "You are El-roi"; for she said, "Have I really seen God and remained alive after seeing him?" [14]Therefore the well was called Beer-lahai-roi; it lies between Kadesh and Bered.

[15]Hagar bore Abram a son; and Abram named his son, whom Hagar bore, Ishmael. [16]Abram was eighty-six years old when Hagar bore him Ishmael.

Reflection

The concern in Genesis 15 over how Abram and the barren Sarai will give birth to a "great nation" continues in this chapter but with significant differences. The Lord does not address Sarai in a vision or within a covenant nor is there the promise of innumerable progeny or a spacious homeland between the great rivers. Instead, she is on her own, as Abram was before the Lord took him in hand.

Earlier, Abram had proposed adopting a slave, Eliezer of Damascus, to be his heir. Now Sarai proposes that her slave-girl, Hagar the Egyptian, have sex with Abram and become her surrogate (16:1-4). The two conceive a child—in some sense a dream come true—but a nightmare ensues. Hagar, victorious in her fertility, becomes contemptuous of Sarai, who is enraged not only at Hagar but also at Abram: "May the Lord judge between you and me!" (16:5). He in turn reacts angrily to both women when he tells Sarai, "Your slave-girl is in your power; do to her as you please" (16:6). By any reckoning, no one in this domestic warfare behaves admirably.

Abused, the pregnant Hagar runs away. At this point, however, the divine enters the human fray. An angel of the Lord—or is it the Lord in disguise?—intervenes directly with Hagar as no heaven emissary did with Sarai. She is told to return and submit to her mistress but is given a promise similar to the one the Lord extended to Abram: "I will so greatly multiply your offspring that they cannot be counted for multitude" (16:10). She will bear a son and call him Ishmael, whose name means "the Lord has given heed."

The author of this narrative says that Hagar called the Lord who intervened *El-ro*i, meaning "the God who sees." Overwhelmed, incredulous, she cries out, "Have I really seen God and remained alive after seeing him?" (16:13). And she has every reason to be amazed, for this "slave-girl" is given intimate access to the Lord that surpasses Sarai and rivals Abram. Her rescue is radiant but not without a shadow. Ishmael will be the forefather of Egypt, the future nemesis of Abram's seed, and in Exodus the enslaver of his offspring. At this foundational moment in human history, however, future enemies begin as brothers. As sons of Abram, *El-roi* has "seen" them both.

— **Dr. Peter S. Hawkins**

Questions

There is little or no idealization in the characters in Genesis. What is the effect of this "warts and all" approach?

The presence of "slaves" in Genesis and the various ways they are "used" in the narrative is disturbing to many readers. How do you deal with problematic issues in scripture?

Prayer

O God, you have always called people into your work who are ignorant of your ways, more blind than farsighted, more sinners than saints. Help us to be caught up in your vision despite our flaws. Work with us as we are, and then make us new. Make us part of your promise. *Amen.*

Genesis 17

17 When Abram was ninety-nine years old, the LORD appeared to Abram, and said to him, "I am God Almighty; walk before me, and be blameless. ²And I will make my covenant between me and you, and will make you exceedingly numerous." ³Then Abram fell on his face; and God said to him,

⁴"As for me, this is my covenant with you: You shall be the ancestor of a multitude of nations. ⁵No longer shall your name be Abram, but your name shall be Abraham; for I have made you the ancestor of a multitude of nations. ⁶I will make you exceedingly fruitful; and I will make nations of you, and kings shall come from you.

⁷I will establish my covenant between me and you, and your offspring after you throughout their generations, for an everlasting covenant, to be God to you and to your offspring after you. ⁸And I will give to you, and to your offspring after you, the land where you are now an alien, all the land of Canaan, for a perpetual holding; and I will be their God." ⁹God said to Abraham, "As for you, you shall keep my covenant, you and your offspring after you throughout their generations. ¹⁰This is my covenant, which you shall keep, between me and you and your offspring after you: Every male among you shall be circumcised. ¹¹You shall circumcise the flesh of your foreskins, and it shall be a sign of the covenant between me and you. ¹²Throughout your generations every male among you shall be circumcised when he is eight days old, including

the slave born in your house and the one bought with your money from any foreigner who is not of your offspring. [13]Both the slave born in your house and the one bought with your money must be circumcised. So shall my covenant be in your flesh an everlasting covenant. [14]Any uncircumcised male who is not circumcised in the flesh of his foreskin shall be cut off from his people; he has broken my covenant."

[15]God said to Abraham, "As for Sarai your wife, you shall not call her Sarai, but Sarah shall be her name. [16]I will bless her, and moreover I will give you a son by her. I will bless her, and she shall give rise to nations; kings of peoples shall come from her." [17]Then Abraham fell on his face and laughed, and said to himself, "Can a child be born to a man who is a hundred years old? Can Sarah, who is ninety years old, bear a child?" [18]And Abraham said to God, "O that Ishmael might live in your sight!" [19]God said, "No, but your wife Sarah shall bear you a son, and you shall name him Isaac. I will establish my covenant with him as an everlasting covenant for his offspring after him. [20]As for Ishmael, I have heard you; I will bless him and make him fruitful and exceedingly numerous; he shall be the father of twelve princes, and I will make him a great nation. [21]But my covenant I will establish with Isaac, whom Sarah shall bear to you at this season next year." [22]And when he had finished talking with him, God went up from Abraham.

[23]Then Abraham took his son Ishmael and all the slaves born in his house or bought with his money, every male among the men of Abraham's house, and he circumcised the flesh of their foreskins that very day, as God had said to him. [24]Abraham

was ninety-nine years old when he was circumcised in the flesh of his foreskin. ²⁵And his son Ishmael was thirteen years old when he was circumcised in the flesh of his foreskin. ²⁶That very day Abraham and his son Ishmael were circumcised; ²⁷and all the men of his house, slaves born in the house and those bought with money from a foreigner, were circumcised with him.

Reflection

A covenant like the one in Genesis 17 transforms us. God singles out Abraham and his descendants to be a witness to God's presence in the world; Abraham in response must accept this covenant and show physically that he is set apart or sanctified for this mission. The word for holy in Hebrew is *Kadosh*, which means separate or consecrated. Thus Abraham must set himself apart from others to affirm his place in God's ethos.

A covenant is different from a contract. When a person signs a contract, there is a buyer and seller, but there is no fundamental change to either individual. When a contract is signed, the two parties remain the same; the only difference is the exchange of goods or services. When a covenant is affirmed, on the other hand, people are transformed. A married couple, for example, establish a covenant between themselves. They are spiritually and physically altered. They can no longer think of the "me," but rather now they must affirm the "we." Just look at the hand of the bride and the groom, and you know instantly by the ring on their finger that they are set apart for each other and no one else. Their hearts and their hands are different.

Likewise, when God establishes a covenant with Abraham and his descendants, they are to change themselves physically. Their faith, lives and bodies are transformed. The text reads, "This is my covenant, which you shall keep, between me and you and your offspring after you: Every male among you shall be circumcised… and it shall be a sign of the covenant between me and you" (Genesis 17:10-11).

Covenants are not easy. They require sacrifice, including the ramifications that come from being different. Rabbi Samson Raphael Hirsch writes, "The establishment of the covenant requires both a physical act that changes the self and a spiritual act. Neither part is complete without the other." Or, to paraphrase Rabbi Abraham Joshua Heschel: "Acts without faith are dead; faith without acts is wild."

— **Rabbi Gregory S. Marx**

Questions

How does our faith change the way we live and interact with the secular world? Does our faith change us in any way?

While ritual circumcision is not required in Christianity, are there other ways that we can circumcise our hearts to affirm the covenant?

Prayer

O Lord our God, set me apart like Abraham and Sarah to be your witness to the world. Give me courage when I am afraid, faith when full of doubt, and strength to live a life covenanted to you. As Abraham bore witness and was changed by the covenant, so may I live a life that physically and spiritually bears witness to my pledge to God. *Amen.*

Genesis 18

18 The LORD appeared to Abraham by the oaks of Mamre, as he sat at the entrance of his tent in the heat of the day. [2]He looked up and saw three men standing near him. When he saw them, he ran from the tent entrance to meet them, and bowed down to the ground. [3]He said, "My LORD, if I find favor with you, do not pass by your servant. [4]Let a little water be brought, and wash your feet, and rest yourselves under the tree. [5]Let me bring a little bread, that you may refresh yourselves, and after that you may pass on—since you have come to your servant." So they said, "Do as you have said." [6]And Abraham hastened into the tent to Sarah, and said, "Make ready quickly three measures of choice flour, knead it, and make cakes." [7]Abraham ran to the herd, and took a calf, tender and good, and gave it to the servant, who hastened to prepare it. [8]Then he took curds and milk and the calf that he had prepared, and set it before them; and he stood by them under the tree while they ate.

[9]They said to him, "Where is your wife Sarah?" And he said, "There, in the tent." [10]Then one said, "I will surely return to you in due season, and your wife Sarah shall have a son." And Sarah was listening at the tent entrance behind him. [11]Now Abraham and Sarah were old, advanced in age; it had ceased to be with Sarah after the manner of women. [12]So Sarah laughed to herself, saying, "After I have grown old, and my husband is old, shall I have pleasure?" [13]The LORD said to Abraham, "Why did Sarah laugh, and say,

'Shall I indeed bear a child, now that I am old?' ¹⁴Is anything too wonderful for the LORD? At the set time I will return to you, in due season, and Sarah shall have a son." ¹⁵But Sarah denied, saying, "I did not laugh"; for she was afraid. He said, "Oh yes, you did laugh."

¹⁶Then the men set out from there, and they looked toward Sodom; and Abraham went with them to set them on their way. ¹⁷The LORD said, "Shall I hide from Abraham what I am about to do, ¹⁸seeing that Abraham shall become a great and mighty nation, and all the nations of the earth shall be blessed in him? ¹⁹No, for I have chosen him, that he may charge his children and his household after him to keep the way of the LORD by doing righteousness and justice; so that the LORD may bring about for Abraham what he has promised him." ²⁰Then the LORD said, "How great is the outcry against Sodom and Gomorrah and how very grave their sin! ²¹I must go down and see whether they have done altogether according to the outcry that has come to me; and if not, I will know." ²²So the men turned from there, and went toward Sodom, while Abraham remained standing before the LORD.

²³Then Abraham came near and said, "Will you indeed sweep away the righteous with the wicked? ²⁴Suppose there are fifty righteous within the city; will you then sweep away the place and not forgive it for the fifty righteous who are in it? ²⁵Far be it from you to do such a thing, to slay the righteous with the wicked, so that the righteous fare as the wicked! Far be that from you! Shall not the Judge of all the earth do what is just?" ²⁶And the LORD said, "If I find at Sodom fifty righteous in the city, I will forgive the whole place for their sake." ²⁷Abraham answered, "Let me

take it upon myself to speak to the LORD, I who am but dust and ashes. [28]Suppose five of the fifty righteous are lacking? Will you destroy the whole city for lack of five?" And he said, "I will not destroy it if I find forty-five there." [29]Again he spoke to him, "Suppose forty are found there." He answered, "For the sake of forty I will not do it." [30]Then he said, "Oh do not let the LORD be angry if I speak. Suppose thirty are found there." He answered, "I will not do it, if I find thirty there." [31]He said, "Let me take it upon myself to speak to the LORD. Suppose twenty are found there." He answered, "For the sake of twenty I will not destroy it." [32]Then he said, "Oh do not let the LORD be angry if I speak just once more. Suppose ten are found there." He answered, "For the sake of ten I will not destroy it." [33]And the LORD went his way, when he had finished speaking to Abraham; and Abraham returned to his place.

Reflection

Genesis 18 is essentially two stories in one. We learn first of the announcement of the birth of Isaac and then we are taken to Sodom and Gomorrah.

Part 1: Three angels tell Abraham and Sarah that God's promise will be fulfilled, and they will have a child. Upon hearing the good news, Sarah cynically mocks the possibility of childbirth. "After I have grown old, and my husband is old, shall I have pleasure?" But the angels remind her of God's great reach: "Is anything too wonderful for the LORD?"

Genesis 18 is the first of 93 miraculous occurrences in the Hebrew Bible. God is known in my Jewish tradition as the *Pele yoetz*, the doer of wonder. Religious faith begins when we look with wonder, fight our cynicism, believe in the wonderment of life, and live with radical amazement.

Part 2: Those same angels who visited Abraham and Sarah now travel to Sodom and Gomorrah with the plan to destroy evil. In this section, Abraham experiences a different kind of wonderment, confronting God and pleading for the lives of the people of Sodom and Gomorrah.

Despite the differences in these two parts of Genesis 18, a common theme emerges. Faith calls us to see the miracle of life, but it does not stop there. With gratitude for the miracles that surround us, our faith is also a transcendent call to work for justice and peace.

Rabbi Abraham Joshua Heschel writes that wonderment leads to engagement. "The beginning of faith is not a feeling for the mystery of living or a sense of awe. The root of religion is the question, what to do with the feeling for the mystery of living. Religion, the end of isolation, begins with a consciousness that something is asked of us…. Wonder is not a state of esthetic enjoyment…. wonder unlocks an innate sense of indebtedness…. The world consists, not of things, but of tasks. Wonder is the state of our being asked."

—**Rabbi Gregory S. Marx**

Questions _____

In what way can our faith help us overcome the ossification of routine and predictability?

How can our faith help us to balance weights and measures with faith and wonderment?

Prayer _____

O God, when I have become ossified under the weight of the same old, same old, may you with a wink and nod call me to open my eyes, my heart, and my mind to the wonderment of life. Help me, O God to live, to fully live, with hope in my heart and wonderment in my soul. When my hope has been cauterized, my vision sealed off, and I am locked in the prison of the now, the polltakers, the analytics, and the bench markers, teach me, lead me to affirm the power of hope and the wonderment of life. *Amen.*

Genesis 19

19 The two angels came to Sodom in the evening, and Lot was sitting in the gateway of Sodom. When Lot saw them, he rose to meet them, and bowed down with his face to the ground. ²He said, "Please, my lords, turn aside to your servant's house and spend the night, and wash your feet; then you can rise early and go on your way." They said, "No; we will spend the night in the square." ³But he urged them strongly; so they turned aside to him and entered his house; and he made them a feast, and baked unleavened bread, and they ate.

⁴But before they lay down, the men of the city, the men of Sodom, both young and old, all the people to the last man, surrounded the house; ⁵and they called to Lot, "Where are the men who came to you tonight? Bring them out to us, so that we may know them." ⁶Lot went out of the door to the men, shut the door after him, ⁷and said, "I beg you, my brothers, do not act so wickedly. ⁸Look, I have two daughters who have not known a man; let me bring them out to you, and do to them as you please; only do nothing to these men, for they have come under the shelter of my roof." ⁹But they replied, "Stand back!" And they said, "This fellow came here as an alien, and he would play the judge! Now we will deal worse with you than with them." Then they pressed hard against the man Lot, and came near the door to break it down. ¹⁰But the men inside reached out their hands and brought Lot into the house with them, and shut the door. ¹¹And they struck with blindness the men who were

at the door of the house, both small and great, so that they were unable to find the door.

¹²Then the men said to Lot, "Have you anyone else here? Sons-in-law, sons, daughters, or anyone you have in the city—bring them out of the place. ¹³For we are about to destroy this place, because the outcry against its people has become great before the LORD, and the LORD has sent us to destroy it." ¹⁴So Lot went out and said to his sons-in-law, who were to marry his daughters, "Up, get out of this place; for the LORD is about to destroy the city." But he seemed to his sons-in-law to be jesting.

¹⁵When morning dawned, the angels urged Lot, saying, "Get up, take your wife and your two daughters who are here, or else you will be consumed in the punishment of the city." ¹⁶But he lingered; so the men seized him and his wife and his two daughters by the hand,

the LORD being merciful to him, and they brought him out and left him outside the city. ¹⁷When they had brought them outside, they said, "Flee for your life; do not look back or stop anywhere in the Plain; flee to the hills, or else you will be consumed." ¹⁸And Lot said to them, "Oh, no, my lords; ¹⁹your servant has found favor with you, and you have shown me great kindness in saving my life; but I cannot flee to the hills, for fear the disaster will overtake me and I die. ²⁰Look, that city is near enough to flee to, and it is a little one. Let me escape there—is it not a little one? — and my life will be saved!" ²¹He said to him, "Very well, I grant you this favor too, and will not overthrow the city of which you have spoken. ²²Hurry, escape there, for I can do nothing until you arrive there." Therefore the city was called Zoar. ²³The sun had risen on the earth when Lot came to Zoar.

²⁴Then the LORD rained on Sodom and Gomorrah sulfur and fire from the LORD out of heaven; ²⁵and he overthrew those cities, and all the Plain, and all the inhabitants of the cities, and what grew on the ground.

²⁶But Lot's wife, behind him, looked back, and she became a pillar of salt.

²⁷Abraham went early in the morning to the place where he had stood before the LORD; ²⁸and he looked down toward Sodom and Gomorrah and toward all the land of the Plain and saw the smoke of the land going up like the smoke of a furnace. ²⁹So it was that, when God destroyed the cities of the Plain, God remembered Abraham, and sent Lot out of the midst of the overthrow, when he overthrew the cities in which Lot had settled.

³⁰Now Lot went up out of Zoar and settled in the hills with his two daughters, for he was afraid to stay in Zoar; so he lived in a cave with his two daughters. ³¹And the firstborn said to the younger, "Our father is old, and there is not a man on earth to come in to us after the manner of all the world. ³²Come, let us make our father drink wine, and we will lie with him, so that we may preserve offspring through our father." ³³So they made their father drink wine that night; and the firstborn went in, and lay with her father; he did not know when she lay down or when she rose. ³⁴On the next day, the firstborn said to the younger, "Look, I lay last night with my father; let us make him drink wine tonight also; then you go in and lie with him, so that we may preserve offspring through our father." ³⁵So they made their father drink wine that night also; and the younger rose, and lay with him; and he did not know when she lay down or when she rose. ³⁶Thus both

the daughters of Lot became pregnant by their father. [37]The firstborn bore a son, and named him Moab; he is the ancestor of the Moabites to this day. [38]The younger also bore a son and named him Ben-ammi; he is the ancestor of the Ammonites to this day.

Reflection

A good friend of mine says, "Jesus is God's language and message to humanity. He is the context of scripture." I could not agree more enthusiastically. Jesus is the lens through which we understand the Bible. Thus, when we engage difficult passages and stories within scripture, we must remember that Jesus Christ provides the perfect context for reading. It is with that foundation that we understand this section of Genesis as well as other passages that appear to show us two very different and contrasting faces of God.

In one of my favorite verses, John 10:10, Jesus says, "The thief comes only to steal and kill and destroy. I came that they may have life, and have it abundantly." Jesus clearly distances himself from an understanding of God as the destroyer and contrasts his action in the world as concerning life, even abundant life.

What then do we do when God appears to be the destroyer on the one hand (in the case of Sodom and Gomorrah) and on the other, the author of our salvation who commands us to bless our enemies and never to return evil for evil? These are important questions with which we must wrestle as followers of Jesus Christ.

One perspective is to consider how the judgment of sin might not be an externally applied penalty directly from God. There is no need for that, if in fact, sin carries its own penalty, as Romans 6:3 reminds us that the wages (or consequences) of sin are death. In this way, occurrences of judgment, like in Genesis 19, potentially do not reflect the heart of God that we see in Jesus. God doesn't actively prosecute, convict, sentence, and condemn sinners.

Ultimately these types of passages challenge us as well as our foundational beliefs about God. As honest students of scripture and disciples, we cannot ignore this tension. Rather, I invite you to discern who God is in light of Jesus. It is the revelation of God's goodness that leads us to repentance; it is not our repentance that leads to God's goodness.

— The Rev. J. Malone Gilliam

Questions _____

When confronted with difficult scripture passages that create tension and contradiction, how do you respond?

Do you find that the core values of your belief are exposed by these instances in the Bible?

Prayer _____

Heavenly Father, you have made yourself fully known in the person of Jesus Christ: We ask for your Spirit to guide us into that truth and encourage us in the knowledge of who you are and who we are in your sight. Give us the assurance of your never-changing, never-failing mercies, which are everlasting from age to age. *Amen.*

Genesis 20

20 From there Abraham journeyed toward the region of the Negeb, and settled between Kadesh and Shur. While residing in Gerar as an alien, ²Abraham said of his wife Sarah, "She is my sister." And King Abimelech of Gerar sent and took Sarah.

³But God came to Abimelech in a dream by night, and said to him, "You are about to die because of the woman whom you have taken; for she is a married woman." ⁴Now Abimelech had not approached her; so he said, "LORD, will you destroy an innocent people? ⁵Did he not himself say to me, 'She is my sister'? And she herself said, 'He is my brother.' I did this in the integrity of my heart and the innocence of my hands." ⁶Then God said to him in the dream, "Yes, I know that you did this in the integrity of your heart; furthermore it was I who kept you from sinning against me. Therefore I did not let you touch her. ⁷Now then, return the man's wife; for he is a prophet, and he will pray for you and you shall live. But if you do not restore her, know that you shall surely die, you and all that are yours."

⁸So Abimelech rose early in the morning, and called all his servants and told them all these things; and the men were very much afraid. ⁹Then Abimelech called Abraham, and said to him, "What have you done to us? How have I sinned against you, that you have brought such great guilt on me and my kingdom? You have done things to me that ought not to be done." ¹⁰And Abimelech said to Abraham, "What were you

thinking of, that you did this thing?" [11]Abraham said, "I did it because I thought, There is no fear of God at all in this place, and they will kill me because of my wife. [12]Besides, she is indeed my sister, the daughter of my father but not the daughter of my mother; and she became my wife. [13]And when God caused me to wander from my father's house, I said to her, 'This is the kindness you must do me: at every place to which we come, say of me, He is my brother.'"

[14]Then Abimelech took sheep and oxen, and male and female slaves, and gave them to Abraham, and restored his wife Sarah to him. [15]Abimelech said, "My land is before you; settle where it pleases you." [16]To Sarah he said, "Look, I have given your brother a thousand pieces of silver; it is your exoneration before all who are with you; you are completely vindicated." [17]Then Abraham prayed to God; and God healed Abimelech, and also healed his wife and female slaves so that they bore children. [18]For the LORD had closed fast all the wombs of the house of Abimelech because of Sarah, Abraham's wife.

Reflection

Looking back over the half century of my life, I can recount times when I see God's hand at work despite my own obstinance, ignorance, and lack of faith. There are more instances of this than I like to admit. What I find so encouraging and glorious is the persistent nature of our Lord to work with me during my messes and the way he seeks to bless me in my sin as well as bless those who have been affected by my sin.

The narrative involving Abraham, Sarah, and Abimelech in this chapter articulates God's graciousness and desire to redeem us and creation. Misjudging the Philistines to be a wicked people, Abraham engages in deception as he presents Sarah as his sister to the Philistine ruler just as he had done with Pharaoh in chapter 12.

Fear motivates Abraham to deal dishonestly with both Pharaoh and Abimelech. It seems easy to understand: his life might very well be in jeopardy before these powerful rulers. Perhaps Abraham remembers God's promise of offspring and is endeavoring to remain alive so the promise may come to fruition. However, despite Abraham's deceptive actions, we come to know him as the "Father of the Faithful."

This is such an amazing reality! The steadfastness of God working creatively in and through the life of Abraham is also at work in my life. My friend and theologian Baxter Kruger likes to describe God's Holy Spirit as a "creative genius" who meets us in our darkness to bring light and redemption.

Honestly, Abraham's tactics hit close to home in my own life. How often have I justified my behavior in the face of fear or expediency?

Too often. Perhaps that's true for all of us. But our faith calls us to focus on our Redeemer Jesus Christ rather than on our failures. God's grace has appeared to keep training us in godliness and truth.

— The Rev. J. Malone Gilliam

Questions

How have you seen the Holy Spirit's creative redemption manifest in your life?

Abraham's attitude toward the Philistines is not dissimilar to Jonah's toward the Ninevites. In both instances, the presumed "ungodly" repent and turn to the Lord. How does that inform your faith? What does it say about God?

Prayer

Almighty Father, we pray for an awareness of your steadfast mercies upon us and the nations around us. Give us compassion for those who differ from us and the strength to engage with them forthrightly. May we also perceive your creative redemption at work in our lives. We ask these things through our Savior Jesus Christ. *Amen.*

Genesis 21

21 The LORD dealt with Sarah as he had said, and the Lord did for Sarah as he had promised. ²Sarah conceived and bore Abraham a son in his old age, at the time of which God had spoken to him. ³Abraham gave the name Isaac to his son whom Sarah bore him. ⁴And Abraham circumcised his son Isaac when he was eight days old, as God had commanded him. ⁵Abraham was a hundred years old when his son Isaac was born to him. ⁶Now Sarah said, "God has brought laughter for me; everyone who hears will laugh with me." ⁷And she said, "Who would ever have said to Abraham that Sarah would nurse children? Yet I have borne him a son in his old age." ⁸The child grew, and was weaned; and Abraham made a great feast on the day that Isaac was weaned.

⁹But Sarah saw the son of Hagar the Egyptian, whom she had borne to Abraham, playing with her son Isaac. ¹⁰So she said to Abraham, "Cast out this slave woman with her son; for the son of this slave woman shall not inherit along with my son Isaac." ¹¹The matter was very distressing to Abraham on account of his son. ¹²But God said to Abraham, "Do not be distressed because of the boy and because of your slave woman; whatever Sarah says to you, do as she tells you, for it is through Isaac that offspring shall be named for you. ¹³As for the son of the slave woman, I will make a nation of him also, because he is your offspring."

¹⁴So Abraham rose early in the morning, and took bread and a skin of water, and gave

it to Hagar, putting it on her shoulder, along with the child, and sent her away. And she departed, and wandered about in the wilderness of Beer-sheba. [15]When the water in the skin was gone, she cast the child under one of the bushes. [16]Then she went and sat down opposite him a good way off, about the distance of a bowshot; for she said, "Do not let me look on the death of the child." And as she sat opposite him, she lifted up her voice and wept. [17]And God heard the voice of the boy; and the angel of God called to Hagar from heaven, and said to her, "What troubles you, Hagar? Do not be afraid; for God has heard the voice of the boy where he is. [18]Come, lift up the boy and hold him fast with your hand, for I will make a great nation of him." [19]Then God opened her eyes and she saw a well of water. She went, and filled the skin with water, and gave the boy a drink. [20]God was with the boy, and he grew up; he lived in the wilderness, and became an expert with the bow. [21]He lived in the wilderness of Paran; and his mother got a wife for him from the land of Egypt.

[22]At that time Abimelech, with Phicol the commander of his army, said to Abraham, "God is with you in all that you do; [23]now therefore swear to me here by God that you will not deal falsely with me or with my offspring or with my posterity, but as I have dealt loyally with you, you will deal with me and with the land where you have resided as an alien." [24]And Abraham said, "I swear it." [25]When Abraham complained to Abimelech about a well of water that Abimelech's servants had seized, [26]Abimelech said, "I do not know who has done this; you did not tell me, and I have not heard of it until today." [27]So Abraham took sheep and oxen and gave them

to Abimelech, and the two men made a covenant. ²⁸Abraham set apart seven ewe lambs of the flock. ²⁹And Abimelech said to Abraham, "What is the meaning of these seven ewe lambs that you have set apart?" ³⁰He said, "These seven ewe lambs you shall accept from my hand, in order that you may be a witness for me that I dug this well." ³¹Therefore that place was called Beer-sheba; because there both of them swore an oath. ³²When they had made a covenant at Beer-sheba, Abimelech, with Phicol the commander of his army, left and returned to the land of the Philistines.

³³Abraham planted a tamarisk tree in Beer-sheba, and called there on the name of the Lord, the Everlasting God. ³⁴And Abraham resided as an alien many days in the land of the Philistines.

Reflection

Genesis 21 contains three distinct stories, joined by the theme of God's faithful dealings with Abraham and his offspring. First, the birth of Isaac fulfills the promise made back in chapter 18 and returns to the theme of laughter from the earlier story promising his arrival (Genesis 18:12-15). "Isaac" in Hebrew is a pun on the word laughter, and in both stories, Sarah laughs, but to very different effect. What she found laughable in the earlier story is now a cause of joy as she exults in the gift of her son.

This happy ending is reminiscent of the reversals of fortune proclaimed by Hannah (1 Samuel 1) and Mary (Luke 1). The change between the two forms of Sarah's laughter is both subtle and profound. Laughter can of course be associated both with derision and delight and reminds us that faith isn't always about changing events or circumstances but about how we receive and interpret them.

In the second story, the complexity of Isaac's arrival is recalled, and another narrative (Genesis 16) recapitulated. The slave Hagar, who had earlier become a proxy for Sarah and had given birth to Abraham's first son Ishmael, is again expelled from Abraham's community, now with her son and this time for good—in both senses of the word. The story is partly an explanation of the origins of different Middle Eastern peoples (Ishmael being the traditional ancestor of the Arabs) but more importantly for us, another instance where God's redemptive action is curious but certain. We can be too quick—as Sarah seems to be—to think that blessings are limited and must be fought over; God cares for Hagar and Ishmael beyond

Sarah's competitive spirit—and also past Abraham's feeble defense of this part of his family.

The last section is a coda to the story of Abraham's dealings with the Philistine king Abimelech (Genesis 20). Again, the passage includes an explanatory element, this time about the name Beer-Sheba, which can mean both "well of the covenant" and "well of seven." The story illustrates the way people, as well as God, engage in peacemaking through covenant and sacrifice, a theme that continues through both testaments and undergirds Jesus's creation of a new covenant with humankind.

— **The Very Rev. Andrew McGowan**

Questions _____

Have you ever found laughter appropriate or necessary to reflect our relationship with God?

When have you discovered that God's care was deeper than you knew or was being expressed in a way different from what you had hoped or expected?

Prayer _____

God of Abraham and Sarah and Hagar, of Isaac and Ishmael, we believe you care for us in ways we know and ways we do not; keep us mindful of your care and generous in our care for others, so that we may be living signs of the love you have for all people; through Christ the maker of our new covenant with you. *Amen.*

Genesis 22

22 After these things God tested Abraham. He said to him, "Abraham!" And he said, "Here I am." [2]He said, "Take your son, your only son Isaac, whom you love, and go to the land of Moriah, and offer him there as a burnt offering on one of the mountains that I shall show you."

[3]So Abraham rose early in the morning, saddled his donkey, and took two of his young men with him, and his son Isaac; he cut the wood for the burnt offering, and set out and went to the place in the distance that God had shown him. [4]On the third day Abraham looked up and saw the place far away. [5]Then Abraham said to his young men, "Stay here with the donkey; the boy and I will go over there; we will worship, and then we will come back to you." [6]Abraham took the wood of the burnt offering and laid it on his son Isaac, and he himself carried the fire and the knife. So the two of them walked on together. [7]Isaac said to his father Abraham, "Father!" And he said, "Here I am, my son." He said, "The fire and the wood are here, but where is the lamb for a burnt offering?" [8]Abraham said, "God himself will provide the lamb for a burnt offering, my son." So the two of them walked on together. [9]When they came to the place that God had shown him, Abraham built an altar there and laid the wood in order. He bound his son Isaac, and laid him on the altar, on top of the wood. [10]Then Abraham reached out his hand and took the knife to kill his son.

[11]But the angel of the LORD called to him from heaven, and

said, "Abraham, Abraham!" And he said, "Here I am." [12]He said, "Do not lay your hand on the boy or do anything to him; for now I know that you fear God, since you have not withheld your son, your only son, from me." [13]And Abraham looked up and saw a ram, caught in a thicket by its horns. Abraham went and took the ram and offered it up as a burnt offering instead of his son. [14]So Abraham called that place "The Lord will provide"; as it is said to this day, "On the mount of the Lord it shall be provided."

[15]The angel of the Lord called to Abraham a second time from heaven, [16]and said, "By myself I have sworn, says the Lord: Because you have done this, and have not withheld your son, your only son, [17]I will indeed bless you, and I will make your offspring as numerous as the stars of heaven and as the sand that is on the seashore. And your offspring shall possess the gate of their enemies, [18]and by your offspring shall all the nations of the earth gain blessing for themselves, because you have obeyed my voice." [19]So Abraham returned to his young men, and they arose and went together to Beer-sheba; and Abraham lived at Beer-sheba.

[20]Now after these things it was told Abraham, "Milcah also has borne children, to your brother Nahor: [21]Uz the firstborn, Buz his brother, Kemuel the father of Aram, [22]Chesed, Hazo, Pildash, Jidlaph, and Bethuel." [23]Bethuel became the father of Rebekah. These eight Milcah bore to Nahor, Abraham's brother. [24]Moreover, his concubine, whose name was Reumah, bore Tebah, Gaham, Tahash, and Maacah.

Reflection

The story of Abraham's near-sacrifice of Isaac is one of the most powerful but also most problematic in scripture. It is not only our modern sensibilities that balk at the ideas that God would command human sacrifice or that the great patriarch Abraham would perform it. Even ancient commentators found themselves scrambling to retrieve the character of one actor at the other's expense: perhaps God didn't mean it, but Abraham was either too credulous or too cowardly, or perhaps God did have a change of mind. Some early interpretations imagined a prologue like that in the Book of Job, where a malicious angel is given permission to stage such a terrible scene to test Abraham, letting God partly off the hook.

It may be that we see all this a little differently if we remember that infant sacrifice was practiced by some of Israel's neighbors and maybe at times by Israelites, too (Micah 6:7). While overall, the voice of scripture condemns the practice vigorously, those who undertook it probably did not see themselves as cruel so much as pious, shocking as this may seem to us. Yet the cruelty of human sacrifice is not really the point of the story, and it is worth reminding ourselves that Isaac is not in fact sacrificed, only a ram is. Sacrifice is a piece of background knowledge that helps us to understand the real point of the story, which was Abraham's obedience and faith.

Living as we do in a society that hides its mammoth and wasteful production of meat from animals and sanctions killings through criminal executions, we should think twice (or three times) before thinking that societies that ritualized similar activities were less humane or wise, or that outrage is the thing we ought to take away from reading the story.

Abraham's steady faith is one thing we do need to ponder, but the other and more important thing is God's faith. Faith in these stories is very much reciprocal and means something more like trust than just belief. Abraham trusts God (Genesis 15:6; Romans 4:3), but God's care for Abraham is more profound than Abraham knows or can imagine. Despite the confronting theme of sacrifice, God's purpose is always to promise and give life.

— **The Very Rev. Andrew McGowan**

Questions

How does the different cultural context of stories like this help or hinder us from understanding and appreciating them?

What does it mean to accept that God has faith in you?

Prayer

God of all that lives, give us true respect and love for all you have made, and show us how to foster the life that is your gift to us, to humankind, and to all creation; we ask this through Jesus Christ, the Life of the World. *Amen.*

Genesis 23

23 Sarah lived one hundred twenty-seven years; this was the length of Sarah's life. ²And Sarah died at Kiriath-arba (that is, Hebron) in the land of Canaan; and Abraham went in to mourn for Sarah and to weep for her.

³Abraham rose up from beside his dead, and said to the Hittites, ⁴"I am a stranger and an alien residing among you; give me property among you for a burying place, so that I may bury my dead out of my sight." ⁵The Hittites answered Abraham, ⁶"Hear us, my Lord; you are a mighty prince among us. Bury your dead in the choicest of our burial places; none of us will withhold from you any burial ground for burying your dead." ⁷Abraham rose and bowed to the Hittites, the people of the land. ⁸He said to them, "If you are willing that I should bury my dead out of my sight, hear me, and entreat for me Ephron son of Zohar, ⁹so that he may give me the cave of Machpelah, which he owns; it is at the end of his field. For the full price let him give it to me in your presence as a possession for a burying place." ¹⁰Now Ephron was sitting among the Hittites; and Ephron the Hittite answered Abraham in the hearing of the Hittites, of all who went in at the gate of his city, ¹¹"No, my lord, hear me; I give you the field, and I give you the cave that is in it; in the presence of my people I give it to you; bury your dead." ¹²Then Abraham bowed down before the people of the land. ¹³He said to Ephron in the hearing of the people of the land, "If you only will listen to me! I will give

the price of the field; accept it from me, so that I may bury my dead there." [14]Ephron answered Abraham, [15]"My lord, listen to me; a piece of land worth four hundred shekels of silver—what is that between you and me? Bury your dead."

[16]Abraham agreed with Ephron; and Abraham weighed out for Ephron the silver that he had named in the hearing of the Hittites, four hundred shekels of silver, according to the weights current among the merchants. [17]So the field of Ephron in Machpelah, which was to the east of Mamre, the field with the cave that was in it and all the trees that were in the field, throughout its whole area, passed [18]to Abraham as a possession in the presence of the Hittites, in the presence of all who went in at the gate of his city. [19]After this, Abraham buried Sarah his wife in the cave of the field of Machpelah facing Mamre (that is, Hebron) in the land of Canaan. [20]The field and the cave that is in it passed from the Hittites into Abraham's possession as a burying place.

Reflection

The great matriarch of the people, Sarah, is dead. Abraham gives full expression to his grief and wants to make sure he does the right thing. At times of death, people often draw close to God, helping to find resolve to chart a path after their loss.

Abraham wants to give Sarah a permanent resting place after a life of so much wandering. But it's complicated. As an immigrant in the land, Abraham is not a property owner. In order to bury Sarah on the land, he must negotiate with the Hittites to purchase what will become the burial site for his wife.

Fortunately, Abraham has a good reputation among the Hittites, and they are willing to work with him so that he can purchase some land. As part of the transaction, they ensure that several witnesses are on hand to witness the negotiation. Eventually they make a deal, and the author of this story details the part of the land that now belongs to Abraham and his descendants. The plot becomes the resting place not only for Sarah but also Abraham, Isaac, Rebecca, Jacob, and Leah.

In my part of the world in Canada, land and property has often not been well negotiated between traditional, indigenous inhabitants and settlers. Too often, colonial governments have bypassed careful processes, breaking trust, sacrificing integrity, and inflicting much suffering. This story from Genesis reminds us there is another way to live together.

Land is about relationship. Contracts and treaties are ways to express that relationship. Even out of the depths of grief and displacement, a good path can be followed on the land, especially when one lives in close relationship with the Creator. The Hittites recognized that Abraham had that close relationship. May all of us so live that we may be recognized by others for having such a relationship with the Creator too.

— The Rev. Jessica Schaap

Questions

What is your attitude toward and experience of either owning or not owning land and property? How does that impact your faith?

When have you had to face a difficult time with lots of complications? Were you able to detect the presence of God through it?

Prayer

Great Creator, help us in all times and in all places. Shape our relationships so that they may be reflections of your good ways in the world. Strengthen our understanding so that we may live with others in ways that are faithful to your example. *Amen*.

Genesis 24

24 Now Abraham was old, well advanced in years; and the LORD had blessed Abraham in all things. [2]Abraham said to his servant, the oldest of his house, who had charge of all that he had, "Put your hand under my thigh [3]and I will make you swear by the LORD, the God of heaven and earth, that you will not get a wife for my son from the daughters of the Canaanites, among whom I live, [4]but will go to my country and to my kindred and get a wife for my son Isaac." [5]The servant said to him, "Perhaps the woman may not be willing to follow me to this land; must I then take your son back to the land from which you came?" [6]Abraham said to him, "See to it that you do not take my son back there. [7]The LORD, the God of heaven, who took me from my father's house and from the land of my birth, and who spoke to me and swore to me, 'To your offspring I will give this land,' he will send his angel before you, and you shall take a wife for my son from there. [8]But if the woman is not willing to follow you, then you will be free from this oath of mine; only you must not take my son back there." [9]So the servant put his hand under the thigh of Abraham his master and swore to him concerning this matter.

[10]Then the servant took ten of his master's camels and departed, taking all kinds of choice gifts from his master; and he set out and went to Aram-naharaim, to the city of Nahor. [11]He made the camels kneel down outside the city by the well of water; it was toward evening, the time when women go out to draw

water. [12]And he said, "O LORD, God of my master Abraham, please grant me success today and show steadfast love to my master Abraham. [13]I am standing here by the spring of water, and the daughters of the townspeople are coming out to draw water. [14]Let the girl to whom I shall say, 'Please offer your jar that I may drink,' and who shall say, 'Drink, and I will water your camels' —let her be the one whom you have appointed for your servant Isaac. By this I shall know that you have shown steadfast love to my master." [15]Before he had finished speaking, there was Rebekah, who was born to Bethuel son of Milcah, the wife of Nahor, Abraham's brother, coming out with her water jar on her shoulder. [16]The girl was very fair to look upon, a virgin, whom no man had known. She went down to the spring, filled her jar, and came up. [17]Then the servant ran to meet her and said, "Please let me sip a little water from your jar." [18]"Drink, my lord," she said, and quickly lowered her jar upon her hand and gave him a drink. [19]When she had finished giving him a drink, she said, "I will draw for your camels also, until they have finished drinking." [20]So she quickly emptied her jar into the trough and ran again to the well to draw, and she drew for all his camels. [21]The man gazed at her in silence to learn whether or not the LORD had made his journey successful. [22]When the camels had finished drinking, the man took a gold nose-ring weighing a half shekel, and two bracelets for her arms weighing ten gold shekels, [23]and said, "Tell me whose daughter you are. Is there room in your father's house for us to spend the night?" [24]She said to him, "I am the daughter of Bethuel son of Milcah, whom she bore to Nahor." [25]She added, "We have plenty of straw and fodder and a place to spend the night." [26]The man bowed his head and worshiped the LORD ²⁷and said, "Blessed be the LORD, the God of my master Abraham, who has not forsaken his steadfast love and his faithfulness toward my master. As for me, the LORD has led me on the way to the house of my master's kin." ²⁸Then the girl ran and told her mother's household about these things.

²⁹Rebekah had a brother whose name was Laban; and Laban ran out to the man, to the spring. ³⁰As soon as he had seen the nose-ring, and the bracelets on his sister's arms, and when he heard the words of his sister Rebekah, "Thus the man spoke to me," he went to the man; and there he was, standing by the camels at the spring. ³¹He said, "Come in, O blessed of the LORD. Why do you stand outside when I have prepared the house and a place for the camels?" ³²So the man came into the house; and Laban unloaded the camels, and gave him straw and fodder for the camels, and water to wash his feet and the

feet of the men who were with him. ³³Then food was set before him to eat; but he said, "I will not eat until I have told my errand." He said, "Speak on." ³⁴So he said, "I am Abraham's servant. ³⁵The LORD has greatly blessed my master, and he has become wealthy; he has given him flocks and herds, silver and gold, male and female slaves, camels and donkeys. ³⁶And Sarah my master's wife bore a son to my master when she was old; and he has given him all that he has. ³⁷My master made me swear, saying, 'You shall not take a wife for my son from the daughters of the Canaanites, in whose land I live; ³⁸but you shall go to my father's house, to my kindred, and get a wife for my son.' ³⁹I said to my master, 'Perhaps the woman will not follow me.' ⁴⁰But he said to me, 'The LORD, before whom I walk, will send his angel with you and make your way successful. You shall get a wife for my son from my kindred, from my father's house. [41]Then you will be free from my oath, when you come to my kindred; even if they will not give her to you, you will be free from my oath.' [42]"I came today to the spring, and said, 'O LORD, the God of my master Abraham, if now you will only make successful the way I am going! [43]I am standing here by the spring of water; let the young woman who comes out to draw, to whom I shall say, "Please give me a little water from your jar to drink," [44]and who will say to me, "Drink, and I will draw for your camels also" —let her be the woman whom the LORD has appointed for my master's son.' [45]"Before I had finished speaking in my heart, there was Rebekah coming out with her water jar on her shoulder; and she went down to the spring, and drew. I said to her, 'Please let me drink.' [46]She quickly let down her jar from her shoulder, and said, 'Drink, and I will also water your camels.' So I drank, and she also watered the camels. [47]Then I asked her, 'Whose daughter are you?' She said, 'The daughter of Bethuel, Nahor's son, whom Milcah bore to him.' So I put the ring on her nose, and the bracelets on her arms. [48]Then I bowed my head and worshiped the LORD, and blessed the LORD, the God of my master Abraham, who had led me by the right way to obtain the daughter of my master's kinsman for his son. [49]Now then, if you will deal loyally and truly with my master, tell me; and if not, tell me, so that I may turn either to the right hand or to the left." [50]Then Laban and Bethuel answered, "The thing comes from the LORD; we cannot speak to you anything bad or good. [51]Look, Rebekah is before you, take her and go, and let her be the wife of your master's son, as the LORD has spoken." [52]When Abraham's servant heard their words, he bowed himself to the ground before the LORD. [53]And the servant brought out jewelry of silver and of gold, and garments, and gave them to Rebekah; he also gave to her brother and to her mother costly ornaments.

⁵⁴Then he and the men who were with him ate and drank, and they spent the night there. When they rose in the morning, he said, "Send me back to my master." ⁵⁵Her brother and her mother said, "Let the girl remain with us a while, at least ten days; after that she may go." ⁵⁶But he said to them, "Do not delay me, since the LORD has made my journey successful; let me go that I may go to my master." ⁵⁷They said, "We will call the girl, and ask her." ⁵⁸And they called Rebekah, and said to her, "Will you go with this man?" She said, "I will." ⁵⁹So they sent away their sister Rebekah and her nurse along with Abraham's servant and his men. ⁶⁰And they blessed Rebekah and said to her, "May you, our sister, become thousands of myriads; may your offspring gain possession of the gates of their foes." ⁶¹Then Rebekah and her maids rose up, mounted the camels, and followed the man; thus the servant took Rebekah, and went his way.

⁶²Now Isaac had come from Beer-lahai-roi, and was settled in the Negeb. ⁶³Isaac went out in the evening to walk in the field; and looking up, he saw camels coming. ⁶⁴And Rebekah looked up, and when she saw Isaac, she slipped quickly from the camel, ⁶⁵and said to the servant, "Who is the man over there, walking in the field to meet us?" The servant said, "It is my master." So she took her veil and covered herself. ⁶⁶And the servant told Isaac all the things that he had done. ⁶⁷Then Isaac brought her into his mother Sarah's tent. He took Rebekah, and she became his wife; and he loved her. So Isaac was comforted after his mother's death.

Reflection

"God moves in mysterious ways, God's wonders to perform." My late mother spoke these words nearly every day of her life. I believe these words—both the part about how God moves and the part about wonders. In truth, every person who seeks to follow God and be a mature spiritual person must accept the not-knowing and seek out the wonders.

Genesis chapter 24 could well be given my mother's words as its chapter heading. We see God acting in mysterious ways, and we see wonders happening in this delightful love story. Nothing makes a love story more memorable than the mystery and the wonder of it.

The story is all about Abraham, the father of faith, exercising his faith in the promises of God. God had promised Abraham that he would be the father of a nation more numerous than the stars of heaven. To fulfill this promise, Abraham's son, Isaac, needed to marry. Abraham sends his servant to find Isaac a wife.

Rebekah, the bride-to-be, who is described as beautiful, shows her character by being generous to strangers. Her act of welcome and hospitality mirrors the action of her future father-in-law, who welcomed three angels who visited him. Not only is Rebekah a generous and beautiful woman, but she is also independent and trusts her own promptings of faith. When it becomes clear that she is the one chosen by God, her family wants her to stay ten days before departing for the land of Abraham, but she insists on leaving the next day. The story ends with her meeting Isaac and Isaac falling deeply in love with her. Later, we see another side of Rebekah, one less flattering. But for now, the Rebekah in this chapter is gracious and loving.

This story has a lot to teach us about our own lives of faith and our readiness to receive the God of love, who moves in mysterious ways and performs wonder. Today, we are called to be like Abraham, a person of complete faith and trust in God. Today, we are called to be servants of God in the way Abraham's trusted servant carried out all the promises he had made to Abraham. Today, we are called to be like Rebekah: willing to serve others, generous to strangers, decisive, and willing to trust a wider design on our lives. Discipleship, in any age, means willingness to leave everything behind to serve God fully, with all the mystery and wonder that come with an evolving spiritual life.

— **The Rev. Dr. Mark Francisco Bozzuti-Jones**

Questions

There are many characters in this story: with whom do you identify the most and the least?

How does this story invite you to pay attention to your faith, your prayer life, and how you make decisions?

Where have you experienced God working in mysterious ways and performing wonders on your faith journey?

Prayer

Faithful God, you move in mysterious ways, and you still perform wonders in our world. Help us to be faithful to your call and give us the grace and courage to serve you with all our hearts, minds, and souls. Give us the spirit of Rebecca that we may always be hospitable and generous, trusting in your wider design on our lives. Help us to serve you without counting the cost. *Amen.*

Genesis 25

25 Abraham took another wife, whose name was Keturah. ²She bore him Zimran, Jokshan, Medan, Midian, Ishbak, and Shuah. ³Jokshan was the father of Sheba and Dedan. The sons of Dedan were Asshurim, Letushim, and Leummim. ⁴The sons of Midian were Ephah, Epher, Hanoch, Abida, and Eldaah. All these were the children of Keturah. ⁵Abraham gave all he had to Isaac. ⁶But to the sons of his concubines Abraham gave gifts, while he was still living, and he sent them away from his son Isaac, eastward to the east country. ⁷This is the length of Abraham's life, one hundred seventy-five years. ⁸Abraham breathed his last and died in a good old age, an old man and full of years, and was gathered to his people. ⁹His sons Isaac and Ishmael buried him in the cave of Machpelah, in the field of Ephron son of Zohar the Hittite, east of Mamre, ¹⁰the field that Abraham purchased from the Hittites. There Abraham was buried, with his wife Sarah.

¹¹After the death of Abraham God blessed his son Isaac. And Isaac settled at Beer-lahai-roi. ¹²These are the descendants of Ishmael, Abraham's son, whom Hagar the Egyptian, Sarah's slave-girl, bore to Abraham. ¹³These are the names of the sons of Ishmael, named in the order of their birth: Nebaioth, the firstborn of Ishmael; and Kedar, Adbeel, Mibsam, ¹⁴Mishma, Dumah, Massa, ¹⁵Hadad, Tema, Jetur, Naphish, and Kedemah. ¹⁶These are the sons of Ishmael and these are their names, by their villages

and by their encampments, twelve princes according to their tribes. [17](This is the length of the life of Ishmael, one hundred thirty-seven years; he breathed his last and died, and was gathered to his people.) [18]They settled from Havilah to Shur, which is opposite Egypt in the direction of Assyria; he settled down alongside of all his people.

[19]These are the descendants of Isaac, Abraham's son: Abraham was the father of Isaac, [20]and Isaac was forty years old when he married Rebekah, daughter of Bethuel the Aramean of Paddan-aram, sister of Laban the Aramean. [21]Isaac prayed to the LORD for his wife, because she was barren; and the LORD granted his prayer, and his wife Rebekah conceived. [22]The children struggled together within her; and she said, "If it is to be this way, why do I live?" So she went to inquire of the LORD. [23]And the LORD said to her, "Two nations are in your womb, and two peoples born of you shall be divided; the one shall be stronger than the other, the elder shall serve the younger." [24]When her time to give birth was at hand, there were twins in her womb. [25]The first came out red, all his body like a hairy mantle; so they named him Esau. [26]Afterward his brother came out, with his hand gripping Esau's heel; so he was named Jacob. Isaac was sixty years old when she bore them. [27]When the boys grew up, Esau was a skillful hunter, a man of the field, while Jacob was a quiet man, living in tents. [28]Isaac loved Esau, because he was fond of game; but Rebekah loved Jacob.

[29]Once when Jacob was cooking a stew, Esau came in from the field, and he was famished. [30]Esau said to Jacob, "Let me eat some of that red stuff, for I am famished!" (Therefore he was called Edom.) [31]Jacob said, "First sell me your birthright."

³²Esau said, "I am about to die; of what use is a birthright to me?" ³³Jacob said, "Swear to me first." So he swore to him, and sold his birthright to Jacob. ³⁴Then Jacob gave Esau bread and lentil stew, and he ate and drank, and rose and went his way. Thus Esau despised his birthright.

Reflection

In this chapter, the story of Abraham comes to its close. We read of the final days of his life and how Abraham cares for and makes provision for the people of his household in the twilight of his life. We also learn that he ultimately passes everything remaining (and it is considerable) to his second son, Isaac.

God does not see the world the same way we do. That seems obvious when you say it, but seeing it in action can be startling. God sees the heart and character of an individual, not the exterior. We see that first with Abraham's sons, Ishmael and Isaac. We see it again and again in the story of his family and his descendants, small and often on the margins but who are the inheritors of God's promise.

Rebekah has two twins, Esau and Jacob. It's not surprising at all that there is conflict between two brothers, even estrangement. But it is surprising to hear God tell Rebekah directly that it will be the second son, not the first, who is heir to the promise God made to the child's grandfather Abraham. At least, this is unexpected news if we don't remember how things turn out when God is around.

Esau seems to have everything a strong community leader should possess, at least in our eyes. Strong, outdoorsy and brave, he is an excellent provider. Jacob is quiet and reserved and beloved of his mother. It's helpful to remember that hunting wasn't held in high esteem in ancient Israel. The description of him as a man who lives in tents is a signal that he's a shepherd. It is Jacob who sees and acts on the opportunity to claim the blessing of his father. And it's this act and Esau's thoughtless response that leads to division and conflict between the descendants—a theme that will arise again and again in Genesis and in the subsequent stories of the descendants of Abraham.

— The Rt. Rev. W. Nicholas Knisely

Questions:

How much of your family's story do you know? Have many generations have been traced? Do you feel like you have a place in that story too? If you don't know your family's story, do you feel like you have a place in the story of God's family?

Have you ever thought that your parents loved one of your siblings more than you? Or your friends cared for each other more than you? Did you ever ask?

Prayer:

God of our family, God of the nations and all peoples, help us to see as you see. Let us not see only the external nature of a person but recognize the inner qualities that our neighbors possess. Let us love your children who live on the margins and in the tents, those who thrive in the wild places and those who do so in domesticity. Do not let our rash decisions and our inability to see the heart cause enmity between within our family and yours. And help us to be reconciled when we do. In Jesus's name and love we pray. *Amen*.

Day 26

Genesis 26

26 Now there was a famine in the land, besides the former famine that had occurred in the days of Abraham. And Isaac went to Gerar, to King Abimelech of the Philistines. [2]The LORD appeared to Isaac and said, "Do not go down to Egypt; settle in the land that I shall show you. [3]Reside in this land as an alien, and I will be with you, and will bless you; for to you and to your descendants I will give all these lands, and I will fulfill the oath that I swore to your father Abraham. [4]I will make your offspring as numerous as the stars of heaven, and will give to your offspring all these lands; and all the nations of the earth shall gain blessing for themselves through your offspring, [5]because Abraham obeyed my voice and kept my charge, my commandments, my statutes, and my laws."

[6]So Isaac settled in Gerar. [7]When the men of the place asked him about his wife, he said, "She is my sister"; for he was afraid to say, "My wife," thinking, "or else the men of the place might kill me for the sake of Rebekah, because she is attractive" in appearance." [8]When Isaac had been there a long time, King Abimelech of the Philistines looked out of a window and saw him fondling his wife Rebekah. [9]So Abimelech called for Isaac, and said, "So she is your wife! Why then did you say, 'She is my sister'?" Isaac said to him, "Because I thought I might die because of her." [10]Abimelech said, "What is this you have done to us? One of the people might easily have lain with your wife,

138

A Journey through Genesis

and you would have brought guilt upon us." [11]So Abimelech warned all the people, saying, "Whoever touches this man or his wife shall be put to death."

[12]Isaac sowed seed in that land, and in the same year reaped a hundredfold. The LORD blessed him, [13]and the man became rich; he prospered more and more until he became very wealthy. [14]He had possessions of flocks and herds, and a great household, so that the Philistines envied him. [15](Now the Philistines had stopped up and filled with earth all the wells that his father's servants had dug in the days of his father Abraham.) [16]And Abimelech said to Isaac, "Go away from us; you have become too powerful for us." [17]So Isaac departed from there and camped in the valley of Gerar and settled there. [18]Isaac dug again the wells of water that had been dug in the days of his father Abraham; for the Philistines had stopped them up after the death of Abraham; and he gave them the names that his father had given them. [19]But when Isaac's servants dug in the valley and found there a well of spring water, [20]the herders of Gerar quarreled with Isaac's herders, saying, "The water is ours." So he called the well Esek, because they contended with him. [21]Then they dug another well, and they quarreled over that one also; so he called it Sitnah. [22]He moved from there and dug another well, and they did not quarrel over it; so he called it Rehoboth, saying, "Now the LORD has made room for us, and we shall be fruitful in the land." [23]From there he went up to Beer-sheba. [24]And that very night the LORD appeared to him and said, "I am the God of your father Abraham; do not be afraid, for I am with you and will bless you and make your offspring numerous for my servant Abraham's sake." [25]So he built an altar there, called

on the name of the Lord, and pitched his tent there. And there Isaac's servants dug a well.

26Then Abimelech went to him from Gerar, with Ahuzzath his adviser and Phicol the commander of his army. 27Isaac said to them, "Why have you come to me, seeing that you hate me and have sent me away from you?" 28They said, "We see plainly that the Lord has been with you; so we say, let there be an oath between you and us, and let us make a covenant with you 29so that you will do us no harm, just as we have not touched you and have done to you nothing but good and have sent you away in peace. You are now the blessed of the Lord." 30So he made them a feast, and they ate and drank. 31In the morning they rose early and exchanged oaths; and Isaac set them on their way, and they departed from him in peace. 32That same day Isaac's servants came and told him about the well that they had dug, and said to him, "We have found water!" 33He called it Shibah; therefore the name of the city is Beer-sheba to this day.

34When Esau was forty years old, he married Judith daughter of Beeri the Hittite, and Basemath daughter of Elon the Hittite; 35and they made life bitter for Isaac and Rebekah.

Reflection

Genesis turns and takes up the stories of Abraham's children and their families. Their stories will seem familiar to us, themes and situations will surface again and again, but how they play out will be different...mostly. The author Samuel Clemens (better known as Mark Twain) is said to have remarked that "history doesn't repeat itself, but it often rhymes."

This chapter of Genesis tells some more of Isaac's story—but not the whole story. Isaac and Rachel's story began in Abraham's story, and the piece here serves to begin the story of the twin brothers Esau and Jacob. Isaac's story, and his entire life, is set in the larger account of Abraham's and Jacob's. Isaac is an important part of the story, but the way it's presented, it's more about his part in their stories. It's not his own story, but it's how his life fits into the story of his family.

Isaac and Rebecca have an experience like Abraham and Sarah did with a powerful person, and following in their footsteps, Isaac tells a lie. But this time, the lie doesn't get out of hand. And, like Abraham and Sarah, Isaac and Rebecca have trouble conceiving a child, but this time the story doesn't turn to a forced relationship with a concubine. This time, there are two children who will be in conflict, but they're twins, not stepbrothers.

Isaac chooses differently, better than his father did. His choices do not mar his story. The choices of his family and the consequences of those choices shape his life, but for his part, he makes the best choice he can make. He is mostly blameless, and he doesn't complain about how other's choices have impacted him. He just does what needs to be done. He gets on with it.

It's striking to me that Isaac's own story isn't the center of our attention. It reminds me that there are people who quietly go about their life doing good and making the best choices that they can, and we don't hear much about them. It's the scandal and the outrage that attract us, not the good. But that's not the case with God.

— **The Rt. Rev. W. Nicholas Knisely**

Questions

Our family often speaks about how certain vocations and certain life patterns appear again and again in our story. Is that true for your family? For you?

Have you ever felt like you were repeating someone else's story? Did your story follow the same path in the end, or was there a change for you? Did you make that change consciously? Did you feel God's presence in those moments?

Prayer

Holy One, God of Abraham, Isaac, and Jacob, and of their families, help us to be like Isaac and Rachel. Help us to do better for ourselves and our loved ones. Help us not to make the same mistakes that so many others have made. Transform us and put a new heart within us that we would turn from our focus on the great and the glorious and see the humble and the good as you see them in your heart. We ask this in the name of your Son, our Savior Jesus. *Amen*.

Genesis 27

27 When Isaac was old and his eyes were dim so that he could not see, he called his elder son Esau and said to him, "My son"; and he answered, "Here I am." ²He said, "See, I am old; I do not know the day of my death. ³Now then, take your weapons, your quiver and your bow, and go out to the field, and hunt game for me. ⁴Then prepare for me savory food, such as I like, and bring it to me to eat, so that I may bless you before I die." ⁵Now Rebekah was listening when Isaac spoke to his son Esau. So when Esau went to the field to hunt for game and bring it, ⁶Rebekah said to her son Jacob, "I heard your father say to your brother Esau, ⁷'Bring me game, and prepare for me savory food to eat, that I may bless you before the LORD before I die.' ⁸Now therefore, my son, obey my word as I command you. ⁹Go to the flock, and get me two choice kids, so that I may prepare from them savory food for your father, such as he likes; ¹⁰and you shall take it to your father to eat, so that he may bless you before he dies." ¹¹But Jacob said to his mother Rebekah, "Look, my brother Esau is a hairy man, and I am a man of smooth skin. ¹²Perhaps my father will feel me, and I shall seem to be mocking him, and bring a curse on myself and not a blessing." ¹³His mother said to him, "Let your curse be on me, my son; only obey my word, and go, get them for me." ¹⁴So he went and got them and brought them to his mother; and his mother prepared savory food, such as his father loved. ¹⁵Then Rebekah took the best garments of her elder son Esau, which

were with her in the house, and put them on her younger son Jacob; ¹⁶and she put the skins of the kids on his hands and on the smooth part of his neck. ¹⁷Then she handed the savory food, and the bread that she had prepared, to her son Jacob.

¹⁸So he went in to his father, and said, "My father"; and he said, "Here I am; who are you, my son?" ¹⁹Jacob said to his father, "I am Esau your firstborn. I have done as you told me; now sit up and eat of my game, so that you may bless me." ²⁰But Isaac said to his son, "How is it that you have found it so quickly, my son?" He answered, "Because the LORD your God granted me success." ²¹Then Isaac said to Jacob, "Come near, that I may feel you, my son, to know whether you are really my son Esau or not." ²²So Jacob went up to his father Isaac, who felt him and said, "The voice is Jacob's voice, but the hands are the hands of Esau."

²³He did not recognize him, because his hands were hairy like his brother Esau's hands; so he blessed him. ²⁴He said, "Are you really my son Esau?" He answered, "I am." ²⁵Then he said, "Bring it to me, that I may eat of my son's game and bless you." So he brought it to him, and he ate; and he brought him wine, and he drank. ²⁶Then his father Isaac said to him, "Come near and kiss me, my son." ²⁷So he came near and kissed him; and he smelled the smell of his garments, and blessed him, and said, "Ah, the smell of my son is like the smell of a field that the LORD has blessed. ²⁸May God give you of the dew of heaven, and of the fatness of the earth, and plenty of grain and wine. ²⁹Let peoples serve you, and nations bow down to you. Be lord over your brothers, and may your mother's sons bow down to you. Cursed be everyone who curses you, and blessed be everyone who blesses you!"

³⁰As soon as Isaac had finished blessing Jacob, when Jacob had scarcely gone out from the presence of his father Isaac, his brother Esau came in from his hunting. ³¹He also prepared savory food, and brought it to his father. And he said to his father, "Let my father sit up and eat of his son's game, so that you may bless me." ³²His father Isaac said to him, "Who are you?" He answered, "I am your firstborn son, Esau." ³³Then Isaac trembled violently, and said, "Who was it then that hunted game and brought it to me, and I ate it all before you came, and I have blessed him? —yes, and blessed he shall be!" ³⁴When Esau heard his father's words, he cried out with an exceedingly great and bitter cry, and said to his father, "Bless me, me also, father!" ³⁵But he said, "Your brother came deceitfully, and he has taken away your blessing." ³⁶Esau said, "Is he not rightly named Jacob? For he has supplanted me these two times. He took away my birthright; and look, now he has taken away my blessing." Then he said, "Have you not reserved a blessing for me?" ³⁷Isaac answered Esau, "I have already made him your lord, and I have given him all his brothers as servants, and with grain and wine I have sustained him. What then can I do for you, my son?" ³⁸Esau said to his father, "Have you only one blessing, father? Bless me, me also, father!" And Esau lifted up his voice and wept. ³⁹Then his father Isaac answered him: "See, away from the fatness of the earth shall your home be, and away from the dew of heaven on high. ⁴⁰By your sword you shall live, and you shall serve your brother; but when you break loose, you shall break his yoke from your neck."

⁴¹Now Esau hated Jacob because of the blessing with which his father had blessed him, and Esau said to himself, "The days

of mourning for my father are approaching; then I will kill my brother Jacob." ⁴²But the words of her elder son Esau were told to Rebekah; so she sent and called her younger son Jacob and said to him, "Your brother Esau is consoling himself by planning to kill you. ⁴³Now therefore, my son, obey my voice; flee at once to my brother Laban in Haran, ⁴⁴and stay with him a while, until your brother's fury turns away— ⁴⁵until your brother's anger against you turns away, and he forgets what you have done to him; then I will send, and bring you back from there. Why should I lose both of you in one day?" ⁴⁶Then Rebekah said to Isaac, "I am weary of my life because of the Hittite women. If Jacob marries one of the Hittite women such as these, one of the women of the land, what good will my life be to me?"

Reflection

Genesis 27 begins with old Isaac's bleary eyes that cannot make out his son in front of his face. He is blind, and his household is a mess.

The story goes like this. Isaac tells his favorite son Esau to go out and hunt and prepare for him the meal he loves so that Isaac can give him a blessing of inheritance. We don't know why the meal is necessary for the blessing, but we know the blessing is big. Isaac's wife, Rebekah, overhears and plots to have their second son, Jacob, disguise himself as Esau and get the blessing for himself. Does she really think this through? Jacob does what she says and utters the brilliant, "I am a smooth man. My brother is a hairy man," to the delight of comedy writers for generations, and is that really the most pressing concern? Apparently it is for the biblical writer, because we get the play by play of how this problem is approached, turning to hairy goat skins. Jacob receives the blessing, and Esau and Isaac are distraught when they figure it out. Rebekah sends Jacob away to spare his life, for the moment.

I struggle with this story because it is so messy. Four clearly defined individuals making their way in tents, together. Is it like Cain and Abel or the Prodigal Son or David's sons or maybe Joseph? Or is it like us, one of us old and bleary eyed, attending to our own loves and needs and missing the needs of our children and spouse? The eager, beloved child of the father, but not of his mother, racing out to earn what he deserves? The mother's beloved child, not sure but not obedient. The mother, destroying her family, or has she always been destroyed? And what was the stew like?

— **The Rev. Winnie Varghese**

Questions

Where are you offended? Can you wonder why?

Do you identify with any of the characters? If so, pray with that part of the story and consider their motivations and the arc of the story to come.

What are the blessings of your life? From whom have they come?

Prayer _____

God, you have created us to be one family. Help us to understand our families, to be strong in who you have made us to be, curious about our relatives who are unjust, and wise with those over whom we have authority. God, make us curious and supportive of children. Clear our eyes and heal our wounds that our trauma may die with us and our hope flourish in generations emerging and all for your glory. *Amen.*

Genesis 28

28 Then Isaac called Jacob and blessed him, and charged him, "You shall not marry one of the Canaanite women. ²Go at once to Paddan-aram to the house of Bethuel, your mother's father; and take as wife from there one of the daughters of Laban, your mother's brother. ³May God Almighty bless you and make you fruitful and numerous, that you may become a company of peoples. ⁴May he give to you the blessing of Abraham, to you and to your offspring with you, so that you may take possession of the land where you now live as an alien—land that God gave to Abraham." ⁵Thus Isaac sent Jacob away; and he went to Paddan-aram, to Laban son of Bethuel the Aramean, the brother of Rebekah, Jacob's and Esau's mother.

⁶Now Esau saw that Isaac had blessed Jacob and sent him away to Paddan-aram to take a wife from there, and that as he blessed him he charged him, "You shall not marry one of the Canaanite women," ⁷and that Jacob had obeyed his father and his mother and gone to Paddan-aram. ⁸So when Esau saw that the Canaanite women did not please his father Isaac, ⁹Esau went to Ishmael and took Mahalath daughter of Abraham's son Ishmael, and sister of Nebaioth, to be his wife in addition to the wives he had.

¹⁰Jacob left Beer-sheba and went toward Haran. ¹¹He came to a certain place and stayed there for the night, because the sun had set. Taking one of the stones of the place, he put it under his head and lay down in that place.

¹²And he dreamed that there was a ladder set up on the earth, the top of it reaching to heaven; and the angels of God were ascending and descending on it. ¹³And the LORD stood beside him and said, "I am the LORD, the God of Abraham your father and the God of Isaac; the land on which you lie I will give to you and to your offspring; ¹⁴and your offspring shall be like the dust of the earth, and you shall spread abroad to the west and to the east and to the north and to the south; and all the families of the earth shall be blessed in you and in your offspring. ¹⁵Know that I am with you and will keep you wherever you go, and will bring you back to this land; for I will not leave you until I have done what I have promised you."

¹⁶Then Jacob woke from his sleep and said, "Surely the LORD is in this place—and I did not know it!" ¹⁷And he was afraid, and said, "How awesome is this place! This is none other than the house of God, and this is the gate of heaven." ¹⁸So Jacob rose early in the morning, and he took the stone that he had put under his head and set it up for a pillar and poured oil on the top of it. ¹⁹He called that place Bethel; but the name of the city was Luz at the first. ²⁰Then Jacob made a vow, saying, "If God will be with me, and will keep me in this way that I go, and will give me bread to eat and clothing to wear, ²¹so that I come again to my father's house in peace, then the LORD shall be my God, ²²and this stone, which I have set up for a pillar, shall be God's house; and of all that you give me I will surely give one tenth to you."

Reflection

After all the scheming, lying, and stealing, Jacob runs away in fear for his life. What happens to his inheritance promised by the blessing he stole from his brother Esau? All the plotting lands him in exile. A sad ending, so we think.

So far, God has been silent. I would have thought that when God finally speaks to Jacob, we would hear words of anger or disappointment. After all, Jacob has lied and deceived. Doesn't he deserve some retribution? At the very least, I would expect God to ask the same question he did of Cain: "Where is your brother? What have you done?" But instead, God gives Jacob a dream, showing him the stairway to heaven with angels ascending and descending! Reams have been written about what this vision means. But I am still stuck on the why. Why does God show him this vision and then promise him even more stuff after all Jacob's bad behavior?

The story of Jacob expresses a fundamental aspect about the relationship between God and humankind. God gives us free will and makes a covenant with us to do good. We mess up. God still loves us and keeps the promise anyway. When we realize God's love and reaffirm our covenant with God, we strengthen our faith, change our way, and then we give back.

— **The Rev. Dr. Eric H. F. Law**

Questions _____

In what ways have you messed up with your God-given free will?

When you are at a low point of your life, how will the presence and promise of God help you move forward?

Prayer _____

O God of Abraham, Sarah, and Hagar, God of Isaac, Rebekah, Jacob, and Esau, God of our redeemer Jesus, through the stories of our ancestors, we learn and acknowledge your unshakable covenant. Help us realize your presence at all times and in all places. Remind us that even when we mess up, you are still there, showing us visions and reaffirming your promise so that we may realign our actions with your dream of justice and peace for the world. *Amen*.

Genesis 29

29 Then Jacob went on his journey, and came to the land of the people of the east. ²As he looked, he saw a well in the field and three flocks of sheep lying there beside it; for out of that well the flocks were watered. The stone on the well's mouth was large, ³and when all the flocks were gathered there, the shepherds would roll the stone from the mouth of the well, and water the sheep, and put the stone back in its place on the mouth of the well. ⁴Jacob said to them, "My brothers, where do you come from?" They said, "We are from Haran." ⁵He said to them, "Do you know Laban son of Nahor?" They said, "We do." ⁶He said to them, "Is it well with him?" "Yes," they replied, "and here is his daughter Rachel, coming with the sheep." ⁷He said, "Look, it is still broad daylight; it is not time for the animals to be gathered together. Water the sheep, and go, pasture them." ⁸But they said, "We cannot until all the flocks are gathered together, and the stone is rolled from the mouth of the well; then we water the sheep."

⁹While he was still speaking with them, Rachel came with her father's sheep; for she kept them. ¹⁰Now when Jacob saw Rachel, the daughter of his mother's brother Laban, and the sheep of his mother's brother Laban, Jacob went up and rolled the stone from the well's mouth, and watered the flock of his mother's brother Laban. ¹¹Then Jacob kissed Rachel, and wept aloud. ¹²And Jacob told Rachel that he was her father's kinsman, and that he was Rebekah's son; and she

ran and told her father. ¹³When Laban heard the news about his sister's son Jacob, he ran to meet him; he embraced him and kissed him, and brought him to his house. Jacob told Laban all these things, ¹⁴and Laban said to him, "Surely you are my bone and my flesh!" And he stayed with him a month.

¹⁵Then Laban said to Jacob, "Because you are my kinsman, should you therefore serve me for nothing? Tell me, what shall your wages be?" ¹⁶Now Laban had two daughters; the name of the elder was Leah, and the name of the younger was Rachel. ¹⁷Leah's eyes were lovely, and Rachel was graceful and beautiful. ¹⁸Jacob loved Rachel; so he said, "I will serve you seven years for your younger daughter Rachel." ¹⁹Laban said, "It is better that I give her to you than that I should give her to any other man; stay with me." ²⁰So Jacob served seven years for Rachel, and they seemed to him but a few days because of the love he had for her. ²¹Then Jacob said to Laban, "Give me my wife that I may go in to her, for my time is completed." ²²So Laban gathered together all the people of the place, and made a feast. ²³But in the evening he took his daughter Leah and brought her to Jacob; and he went in to her. ²⁴(Laban gave his maid Zilpah to his daughter Leah to be her maid.) ²⁵When morning came, it was Leah! And Jacob said to Laban, "What is this you have done to me? Did I not serve with you for Rachel? Why then have you deceived me?" ²⁶Laban said, "This is not done in our country—giving the younger before the firstborn. ²⁷Complete the week of this one, and we will give you the other also in return for serving me another seven years." ²⁸Jacob did so, and completed her week; then Laban gave him his daughter Rachel as a wife. ²⁹(Laban gave

his maid Bilhah to his daughter Rachel to be her maid.) ³⁰So Jacob went in to Rachel also, and he loved Rachel more than Leah. He served Laban for another seven years.

³¹When the LORD saw that Leah was unloved, he opened her womb; but Rachel was barren. ³²Leah conceived and bore a son, and she named him Reuben; for she said, "Because the LORD has looked on my affliction; surely now my husband will love me." ³³She conceived again and bore a son, and said, "Because the LORD has heard that I am hated, he has given me this son also"; and she named him Simeon. ³⁴Again she conceived and bore a son, and said, "Now this time my husband will be joined to me, because I have borne him three sons"; therefore he was named Levi. ³⁵She conceived again and bore a son, and said, "This time I will praise the LORD"; therefore she named him Judah; then she ceased bearing.

Reflection

Jacob falls in love with Rachel and is given Leah. When Jacob wakes up the next morning, he feels cheated, but how does Leah feel? The text doesn't tell us, but the names she gives to her sons provide some insight.

Leah's first three sons are named Reuben (meaning "behold a son"), Simeon (meaning "hearing"), and Levi (meaning "to be joined"). Each of their names focus on the hope that she has for her relationship with Jacob. Reuben grows, and Jacob does not love her. Simeon comes, and Leah still feels hated. When Levi, the third son, comes along, she still longs for connection with Jacob.

But then there's a shift in how Leah names her sons. She names the next baby she brings into the world Judah (meaning "praise"), as a way to praise the Lord. When her handmaid, Zilpah, bears children for Jacob, she calls Gad good fortune, and Asher, happy. This is in stark contrast to Rachel, who is envious and names Dan and Naphtali for judgment and struggle. Despite the unhappy situation in which Leah finds herself, her focus has moved from finding meaning and belovedness with Jacob—it becomes painfully clear that no number of sons will bring his love—to finding her blessedness in God.

So often we chase meaning and love in relationships that cannot give us the belovedness that we crave. We pour time and energy into seeking the approval and affection of others, allowing what we need to really live slip through our fingers. Even a perfect partner or a perfect sister can never fulfill our deep need to be loved for who we are. Instead, like Leah, we can turn our eyes toward the good gifts, blessedness, and love that God gives us. When Leah turned her eyes to God, she found happiness, good fortune, and, despite everything she went through, celebration of God.

— **The Rev. Canon Becky Zartman**

A Journey through Genesis

Questions

Are you looking for something that cannot be found? What is it?

In what ways is God already blessing you?

How can you remind yourself of these blessings throughout your day?

Prayer

God of all good things, Creator of love and source of life, you know our deepest longings and desires before we can name them. Help us to see the gifts that you have already given us, help us to grow in your love, and like Leah, help us to learn to praise your name. *Amen.*

Genesis 30

30 When Rachel saw that she bore Jacob no children, she envied her sister; and she said to Jacob, "Give me children, or I shall die!" [2]Jacob became very angry with Rachel and said, "Am I in the place of God, who has withheld from you the fruit of the womb?" [3]Then she said, "Here is my maid Bilhah; go in to her, that she may bear upon my knees and that I too may have children through her." [4]So she gave him her maid Bilhah as a wife; and Jacob went in to her. [5]And Bilhah conceived and bore Jacob a son. [6]Then Rachel said, "God has judged me, and has also heard my voice and given me a son"; therefore she named him Dan. [7]Rachel's maid Bilhah conceived again and bore Jacob a second son. [8]Then Rachel said, "With mighty wrestlings I have wrestled with my sister, and have prevailed"; so she named him Naphtali. [9]When Leah saw that she had ceased bearing children, she took her maid Zilpah and gave her to Jacob as a wife. [10]Then Leah's maid Zilpah bore Jacob a son. [11]And Leah said, "Good fortune!" so she named him Gad. [12]Leah's maid Zilpah bore Jacob a second son. [13]And Leah said, "Happy am I! For the women will call me happy"; so she named him Asher.

[14]In the days of wheat harvest Reuben went and found mandrakes in the field, and brought them to his mother Leah. Then Rachel said to Leah, "Please give me some of your son's mandrakes." [15]But she said to her, "Is it a small matter that you have taken away my husband? Would you take away my son's mandrakes also?" Rachel said, "Then he may lie with you tonight for

your son's mandrakes." ¹⁶When Jacob came from the field in the evening, Leah went out to meet him, and said, "You must come in to me; for I have hired you with my son's mandrakes." So he lay with her that night. ¹⁷And God heeded Leah, and she conceived and bore Jacob a fifth son. ¹⁸Leah said, "God has given me my hire because I gave my maid to my husband"; so she named him Issachar. ¹⁹And Leah conceived again, and she bore Jacob a sixth son. ²⁰Then Leah said, "God has endowed me with a good dowry; now my husband will honor me, because I have borne him six sons"; so she named him Zebulun. ²¹Afterwards she bore a daughter, and named her Dinah. ²²Then God remembered Rachel, and God heeded her and opened her womb. ²³She conceived and bore a son, and said, "God has taken away my reproach"; ²⁴and she named him Joseph, saying, "May the LORD add to me another son!"

²⁵When Rachel had borne Joseph, Jacob said to Laban, "Send me away, that I may go to my own home and country. ²⁶Give me my wives and my children for whom I have served you, and let me go; for you know very well the service I have given you." ²⁷But Laban said to him, "If you will allow me to say so, I have learned by divination that the LORD has blessed me because of you; ²⁸name your wages, and I will give it." ²⁹Jacob said to him, "You yourself know how I have served you, and how your cattle have fared with me. ³⁰For you had little before I came, and it has increased abundantly; and the LORD has blessed you wherever I turned. But now when shall I provide for my own household also?" ³¹He said, "What shall I give you?" Jacob said, "You shall not give me anything; if you will do this for me, I will again feed your flock and keep it: ³²let me pass through all your flock today, removing from it every speckled

and spotted sheep and every black lamb, and the spotted and speckled among the goats; and such shall be my wages. ³³So my honesty will answer for me later, when you come to look into my wages with you. Every one that is not speckled and spotted among the goats and black among the lambs, if found with me, shall be counted stolen." ³⁴Laban said, "Good! Let it be as you have said." ³⁵But that day Laban removed the male goats that were striped and spotted, and all the female goats that were speckled and spotted, every one that had white on it, and every lamb that was black, and put them in charge of his sons; ³⁶and he set a distance of three days' journey between himself and Jacob, while Jacob was pasturing the rest of Laban's flock.

³⁷Then Jacob took fresh rods of poplar and almond and plane, and peeled white streaks in them, exposing the white of the rods. ³⁸He set the rods that he had peeled in front of the flocks in the troughs, that is, the watering places, where the flocks came to drink. And since they bred when they came to drink, ³⁹the flocks bred in front of the rods, and so the flocks produced young that were striped, speckled, and spotted. ⁴⁰Jacob separated the lambs, and set the faces of the flocks toward the striped and the completely black animals in the flock of Laban; and he put his own droves apart, and did not put them with Laban's flock. ⁴¹Whenever the stronger of the flock were breeding, Jacob laid the rods in the troughs before the eyes of the flock, that they might breed among the rods, ⁴²but for the feebler of the flock he did not lay them there; so the feebler were Laban's, and the stronger Jacob's. ⁴³Thus the man grew exceedingly rich, and had large flocks, and male and female slaves, and camels and donkeys.

Reflection

Laban and Jacob strike (another) deal. Jacob will tend all of Laban's flocks in return for the speckled animals. But Laban soon breaks (another) promise. Instead of giving Jacob his whole herd, he hides his speckled animals from Jacob. In return, Jacob works to propagate stronger and larger flocks than Laban—and succeeds. All the while, what both men are best at breeding is resentment for one another.

It didn't have to be that way. It never had to be this way.

When Laban and Jacob settle on a wage, they're not talking about the animals Laban has right now but rather the animals Laban will have in the future, assuming Jacob does a good job tending Laban's flocks. Jacob's offer costs Laban nothing but potential. But Laban feels the need to take away even that from Jacob. Laban is so worried about losing potential goats that he is willing to double-cross his nephew to get ahead, again.

It's easy to point fingers at Laban, and yet we play this game, too. We interact with the world as if it is a zero-sum game. Someone else gets a promotion, and it feels like it was taken away from us. If she gets into that college, she's taken my spot. We jealously guard our future earnings on the stock market, trying to win out over other investors. Like Laban, we tend to buy into the idea that if Jacob wins, Laban loses, and if Jacob loses, Laban wins. In reality, *there aren't even any goats yet.*

The God of Abraham, Isaac, and Jacob is a God who creates, who calls that creation good and who makes that creation good. When we live as though someone else must lose in order for us to win, it is a failure of imagination, a failure to trust that God will provide enough for everyone. It doesn't have to be that way. It never has to be this way.

— The Rev. Canon Becky Zartman

Questions _____

What are your imaginary goats? Why are they important to you?

What feels like a zero-sum game in your own life right now?

Can you imagine a bigger solution than winning or losing?

Prayer _____

God of flocks and herds and abundance, God of creation and imagination, God of possibility and promise, the world you created is far bigger than we can ever know. Help us to catch a glimpse of this truth and to care for each other. *Amen.*

Genesis 31

31 Now Jacob heard that the sons of Laban were saying, "Jacob has taken all that was our father's; he has gained all this wealth from what belonged to our father." ²And Jacob saw that Laban did not regard him as favorably as he did before. ³Then the Lord said to Jacob, "Return to the land of your ancestors and to your kindred, and I will be with you." ⁴So Jacob sent and called Rachel and Leah into the field where his flock was, ⁵and said to them, "I see that your father does not regard me as favorably as he did before. But the God of my father has been with me. ⁶You know that I have served your father with all my strength; ⁷yet your father has cheated me and changed my wages ten times, but God did not permit him to harm me. ⁸If he said, 'The speckled shall be your wages,' then all the flock bore speckled; and if he said, 'The striped shall be your wages,' then all the flock bore striped. ⁹Thus God has taken away the livestock of your father, and given them to me. ¹⁰During the mating of the flock I once had a dream in which I looked up and saw that the male goats that leaped upon the flock were striped, speckled, and mottled. ¹¹Then the angel of God said to me in the dream, 'Jacob,' and I said, 'Here I am!' ¹²And he said, 'Look up and see that all the goats that leap on the flock are striped, speckled, and mottled; for I have seen all that Laban is doing to you. ¹³I am the God of Bethel, where you anointed a pillar and made a vow to me. Now leave this land at once and return to the land of your birth.'" ¹⁴Then Rachel and Leah answered him, "Is there any portion or inheritance left to us in our father's house? [15]Are we not regarded by him as foreigners? For he has sold us, and he has been using up the money given for us. [16]All the property that God has taken away from our father belongs to us and to our children; now then, do whatever God has said to you."

[17]So Jacob arose, and set his children and his wives on camels; [18]and he drove away all his livestock, all the property that he had gained, the livestock in his possession that he had acquired in Paddan-aram, to go to his father Isaac in the land of Canaan. [19]Now Laban had gone to shear his sheep, and Rachel stole her father's household gods. [20]And Jacob deceived Laban the Aramean, in that he did not tell him that he intended to flee. [21]So he fled with all that he had; starting out

he crossed the Euphrates, and set his face toward the hill country of Gilead. [22]On the third day Laban was told that Jacob had fled. [23]So he took his kinsfolk with him and pursued him for seven days until he caught up with him in the hill country of Gilead. [24]But God came to Laban the Aramean in a dream by night, and said to him, "Take heed that you say not a word to Jacob, either good or bad."

[25]Laban overtook Jacob. Now Jacob had pitched his tent in the hill country, and Laban with his kinsfolk camped in the hill country of Gilead. [26]Laban said to Jacob, "What have you done? You have deceived me, and carried away my daughters like captives of the sword. [27]Why did you flee secretly and deceive me and not tell me? I would have sent you away with mirth and songs, with tambourine and lyre. [28]And why did you not permit me to kiss my sons and

my daughters farewell? What you have done is foolish. ²⁹It is in my power to do you harm; but the God of your father spoke to me last night, saying, 'Take heed that you speak to Jacob neither good nor bad.' ³⁰Even though you had to go because you longed greatly for your father's house, why did you steal my gods?" ³¹Jacob answered Laban, "Because I was afraid, for I thought that you would take your daughters from me by force. ³²But anyone with whom you find your gods shall not live. In the presence of our kinsfolk, point out what I have that is yours, and take it." Now Jacob did not know that Rachel had stolen the gods. ³³So Laban went into Jacob's tent, and into Leah's tent, and into the tent of the two maids, but he did not find them. And he went out of Leah's tent, and entered Rachel's. ³⁴Now Rachel had taken the household gods and put them in the camel's saddle, and sat on them. Laban felt all about in the tent, but did not find them. ³⁵And she said to her father, "Let not my LORD be angry that I cannot rise before you, for the way of women is upon me." So he searched, but did not find the household gods.

³⁶Then Jacob became angry, and upbraided Laban. Jacob said to Laban, "What is my offense? What is my sin, that you have hotly pursued me? ³⁷Although you have felt about through all my goods, what have you found of all your household goods? Set it here before my kinsfolk and your kinsfolk, so that they may decide between us two. ³⁸These twenty years I have been with you; your ewes and your female goats have not miscarried, and I have not eaten the rams of your flocks. ³⁹That which was torn by wild beasts I did not bring to you; I bore the loss of it myself; of my hand you required it, whether stolen by day or stolen by night. ⁴⁰It was like this with

me: by day the heat consumed me, and the cold by night, and my sleep fled from my eyes. [41]These twenty years I have been in your house; I served you fourteen years for your two daughters, and six years for your flock, and you have changed my wages ten times. [42]If the God of my father, the God of Abraham and the Fear of Isaac, had not been on my side, surely now you would have sent me away empty-handed. God saw my affliction and the labor of my hands, and rebuked you last night."

[43]Then Laban answered and said to Jacob, "The daughters are my daughters, the children are my children, the flocks are my flocks, and all that you see is mine. But what can I do today about these daughters of mine, or about their children whom they have borne? [44]Come now, let us make a covenant, you and I; and let it be a witness between you and me." [45]So Jacob took a stone, and set it up as a pillar. [46]And Jacob said to his kinsfolk, "Gather stones," and they took stones, and made a heap; and they ate there by the heap. [47]Laban called it Jegar-sahadutha: but Jacob called it Galeed. [48]Laban said, "This heap is a witness between you and me today." Therefore he called it Galeed, [49]and the pillar Mizpah, for he said, "The LORD watch between you and me, when we are absent one from the other. [50]If you ill-treat my daughters, or if you take wives in addition to my daughters, though no one else is with us, remember that God is witness between you and me." [51]Then Laban said to Jacob, "See this heap and see the pillar, which I have set between you and me. [52]This heap is a witness, and the pillar is a witness, that I will not pass beyond this heap to you, and you will not pass beyond this heap and this pillar to me, for harm. [53]May the God of Abraham and the God

of Nahor"— the God of their father— "judge between us." So Jacob swore by the Fear of his father Isaac, [54]and Jacob offered a sacrifice on the height and called his kinsfolk to eat bread; and they ate bread and tarried all night in the hill country. [55]Early in the morning Laban rose up, and kissed his grandchildren and his daughters and blessed them; then he departed and returned home.

Reflection

Jacob's life is framed by struggles with three characters. The first is his twin, Esau, who the "heel-grabber" (Genesis 25:26) keeps tripping up, swindling him of his birthright for a bowl of beans and later conspiring with their mother Rebekah to steal a blessing from their father Isaac. Fearful of Esau, Jacob goes on the lam from his homeland and joins his uncle Laban's household in Syria.

Jacob's second struggle is with Laban, who outsmarts Jacob by marrying him to his firstborn Leah and indenturing Jacob for a second seven-year hitch to marry Rachel. This nephew and uncle engage in two decades of trickster competition: in Genesis 29, Laban pulls a nuptial switcheroo on Jacob, and in Genesis 30, Jacob literally and figuratively fleeces Laban.

Genesis 31 narrates the end of Jacob's sojourn in Syria and marks the end of his struggle with Laban, highlighting the same themes as in the Esau traditions: deception, alienation, flight, and reconciliation. Their mutual deceptions are alluded to: Jacob claims Laban had repeatedly "cheated" him (Genesis 31:7); Laban claims Jacob had "deceived" him (31:27). Jacob flees with Laban's daughters and flocks, with Laban and his sons in pursuit. When the two parties finally encounter each other, the rivals make peace and erect a memorial cairn to commemorate their covenant and serve as a boundary marker.

Rachel provides a final note of comic tension to the chapter. Unbeknownst to Jacob, she has stolen valuables from her father, his *teraphim*, statuette-like icons that represented the ancestors and whose possession symbolized clan leadership. Jacob inadvertently puts his wife in peril when, in response to Laban's charge that Jacob has stolen his sacred objects and sure of his own innocence, he vows that anyone in his group found with the icons be killed. But Rachel places the objects under her saddle and when approached by Laban, apologizes for not dismounting from her donkey since she's menstruating. Daddy leaves her saddlebags unsearched. And what of the third character with whom Jacob struggles? For that, we must turn to Genesis 32.

— The Rev. Dr. Gregory Mobley

Questions

Do we, like Jacob with Esau and with Laban, find ourselves repeating the same scenarios in different relationships throughout our lives?

Jacob never graduates from his trickster personality, yet God never abandons him. In that light, should we affirm our quirks and flaws and, with humor and humility, press on toward faithfulness to our callings?

Prayer

Morning by morning, O Divine Parent, may we like Laban's grandchildren experience your kisses, and like Laban's daughters, your blessing. *Amen.*

Genesis 32

32 Jacob went on his way and the angels of God met him; ²and when Jacob saw them he said, "This is God's camp!" So he called that place Mahanaim.

³Jacob sent messengers before him to his brother Esau in the land of Seir, the country of Edom, ⁴instructing them, "Thus you shall say to my lord Esau: Thus says your servant Jacob, 'I have lived with Laban as an alien, and stayed until now; ⁵and I have oxen, donkeys, flocks, male and female slaves; and I have sent to tell my lord, in order that I may find favor in your sight.'" ⁶The messengers returned to Jacob, saying, "We came to your brother Esau, and he is coming to meet you, and four hundred men are with him." ⁷Then Jacob was greatly afraid and distressed; and he

divided the people that were with him, and the flocks and herds and camels, into two companies, ⁸thinking, "If Esau comes to the one company and destroys it, then the company that is left will escape."

⁹And Jacob said, "O God of my father Abraham and God of my father Isaac, O LORD who said to me, 'Return to your country and to your kindred, and I will do you good,' ¹⁰I am not worthy of the least of all the steadfast love and all the faithfulness that you have shown to your servant, for with only my staff I crossed this Jordan; and now I have become two companies. ¹¹Deliver me, please, from the hand of my brother, from the hand of Esau, for I am afraid of him; he may come and kill us all, the mothers with the children. ¹²Yet you have said, 'I will surely do you good,

and make your offspring as the sand of the sea, which cannot be counted because of their number.'"

[13]So he spent that night there, and from what he had with him he took a present for his brother Esau, [14]two hundred female goats and twenty male goats, two hundred ewes and twenty rams, [15]thirty milch camels and their colts, forty cows and ten bulls, twenty female donkeys and ten male donkeys. [16]These he delivered into the hand of his servants, every drove by itself, and said to his servants, "Pass on ahead of me, and put a space between drove and drove." [17]He instructed the foremost, "When Esau my brother meets you, and asks you, 'To whom do you belong? Where are you going? And whose are these ahead of you?' [18]then you shall say, 'They belong to your servant Jacob; they are a present sent to my lord Esau; and moreover he is behind us.'" [19]He likewise instructed the second and the third and all who followed the droves, "You shall say the same thing to Esau when you meet him, [20]and you shall say, 'Moreover your servant Jacob is behind us.'" For he thought, "I may appease him with the present that goes ahead of me, and afterwards I shall see his face; perhaps he will accept me." [21]So the present passed on ahead of him; and he himself spent that night in the camp. [22]The same night he got up and took his two wives, his two maids, and his eleven children, and crossed the ford of the Jabbok. [23]He took them and sent them across the stream, and likewise everything that he had.

[24]Jacob was left alone; and a man wrestled with him until daybreak. [25]When the man saw that he did not prevail against Jacob, he struck him on the hip socket; and Jacob's hip was put out of joint as he wrestled with him. [26]Then he said, "Let me go, for the day is breaking." But

Jacob said, "I will not let you go, unless you bless me." ²⁷So he said to him, "What is your name?" And he said, "Jacob." ²⁸Then the man said, "You shall no longer be called Jacob, but Israel, for you have striven with God and with humans, and have prevailed." ²⁹Then Jacob asked him, "Please tell me your name." But he said, "Why is it that you ask my name?" And there he blessed him. ³⁰So Jacob called the place Peniel, saying, "For I have seen God face to face, and yet my life is preserved." ³¹The sun rose upon him as he passed Penuel, limping because of his hip. ³²Therefore to this day the Israelites do not eat the thigh muscle that is on the hip socket, because he struck Jacob on the hip socket at the thigh muscle.

Reflection

As noted in the commentary on Genesis 31, Jacob's life is framed by struggles with three characters: his brother Esau and uncle Laban are two. The third, as demonstrated in the haunting scene in Genesis 32:22–32, is God.

Having reconciled his rivalry with Laban in the preceding chapter, the first two-thirds of Genesis 32 concern Jacob's fearful preparations for an encounter with Esau, the brother whom he had cheated out of birthright and blessing. After living in exile for 20 years, Jacob, along with his wives and children, is finally headed home, to Canaan and his aged father Isaac. But before Jacob—so utterly different from when he last was home—can experience the future he has dreamed of, he must face a reckoning with his past.

When he hears that Esau with a company of 400 men is headed to intercept him before he reaches the Jordan, Jacob mistakenly assumes it is a war party and takes defensive measures: dividing his group to minimize losses from an attack and sending waves of livestock ahead of him to appease Esau with gifts.

Then we have the baffling scene at the Jabbok. In the haze of a midnight river bottom, Jacob is attacked. But by whom? Is it a man? An angel? Some kind of nocturnal demon that must crawl back into its lair before sunrise? According to Hosea 12:3–4 and Genesis 32:28–30, his adversary is God.

Here we have the Bible's archetypal portrayal of heroism. Jacob—eponymous of Israel itself— triumphs not because he is stronger, wiser, or more righteous than his opponent but because of spiritual tenacity. Wounded Jacob refuses to let go of this experience, no matter how arduous, until he receives a blessing from his pain.

This spooky story represents another biblical scene in which faith entails wrestling with God. The biblical God seems to invite bold questioning, as when Abraham bargains with God over the fate of Sodom, Moses urges God to turn back from anger after the golden calf episode, or Jesus—sweating beads of blood—pleads in Gethsemane to be spared the bitter cup.

— **The Rev. Dr. Gregory Mobley**

Questions _____

Have you, like Jacob, had difficult nights of the soul? Like Jacob with his limp, do you bear spiritual scars?

Jacob received "a blessing from his pain," which is not a passive, facile acceptance of trauma ("It must have God's will") but the difficult soul-work of mining even negative experiences for the gold of meaning and insight. How does this idea resonate in you?

Prayer _____

God of Infinite Mystery, whose face we see in a mirror dimly, whose name and essence we know in part, help us endure and bear all things until that glad morning when dawns never-ending love. *Amen.*

Genesis 33

33 Now Jacob looked up and saw Esau coming, and four hundred men with him. So he divided the children among Leah and Rachel and the two maids. ²He put the maids with their children in front, then Leah with her children, and Rachel and Joseph last of all. ³He himself went on ahead of them, bowing himself to the ground seven times, until he came near his brother. ⁴But Esau ran to meet him, and embraced him, and fell on his neck and kissed him, and they wept.

⁵When Esau looked up and saw the women and children, he said, "Who are these with you?" Jacob said, "The children whom God has graciously given your servant." ⁶Then the maids drew near, they and their children, and bowed down; ⁷Leah likewise and her children drew near and bowed down; and finally Joseph and Rachel drew near, and they bowed down. ⁸Esau said, "What do you mean by all this company that I met?" Jacob answered, "To find favor with my lord." ⁹But Esau said, "I have enough, my brother; keep what you have for yourself." ¹⁰Jacob said, "No, please; if I find favor with you, then accept my present from my hand; for truly to see your face is like seeing the face of God—since you have received me with such favor. ¹¹Please accept my gift that is brought to you, because God has dealt graciously with me, and because I have everything I want." So he urged him, and he took it. ¹²Then Esau said, "Let us journey on our way, and I will go alongside you." ¹³But Jacob said to him, "My lord knows that the children are frail

and that the flocks and herds, which are nursing, are a care to me; and if they are overdriven for one day, all the flocks will die. [14]Let my lord pass on ahead of his servant, and I will lead on slowly, according to the pace of the cattle that are before me and according to the pace of the children, until I come to my lord in Seir." [15]So Esau said, "Let me leave with you some of the people who are with me." But he said, "Why should my lord be so kind to me?"

[16]So Esau returned that day on his way to Seir. [17]But Jacob journeyed to Succoth, and built himself a house, and made booths for his cattle; therefore the place is called Succoth. [18]Jacob came safely to the city of Shechem, which is in the land of Canaan, on his way from Paddan-aram; and he camped before the city. [19]And from the sons of Hamor, Shechem's father, he bought for one hundred pieces of money the plot of land on which he had pitched his tent. [20]There he erected an altar and called it El-Elohe-Israel.

Reflection

A lot has already happened. A lot is still ahead. Jacob finds himself, as if on a fulcrum, teetering between his past and future. In this passage, we find him in the present, alone and unsure. The past is plenty complicated: having stolen his father Isaac's blessing from his brother Esau, Jacob had to flee for his life. In that exile, he made his way, building a successful life for himself: two wives, twelve sons, and one daughter, servants, slaves (yes, there were slaves), and plenty of livestock. He didn't acquire all that by the most scrupulous of means but acquire it he did. But home called to him, and he was journeying back to Canaan.

Fearful of his brother Esau's reaction, he kept all that he loved and possessed back behind him. The night before the brothers' reunion, he encountered an angel/a man/God's very self, and they wrestled until dawn. Jacob received a new name (Israel), a blessing, and a permanently disjointed hip. It changed him, but how much?

Jacob's story is both exotic and perfectly prosaic. Despite a profound experience of the holy, all Jacob, now Israel, can imagine as he approaches Esau is what he would do if the situation was reversed. He would seek revenge and the settling of scores. That possibility is terrifying and all he can envision.

Esau has chosen another way, refusing to let the past and the injury done to him constrain his future. Perhaps Esau most remembers a twin brother he loved and played with, but whatever the reason, from the abundance of his life and with a grace-filled spirit he embraces Jacob, knowing that in God there is room and blessing for them both.

Jacob remains dubious even as Esau offers both an embrace and protection for Jacob's travels. Accepting Jacob's need to make his own way (to a new land, to grace, to trust?) Esau departs. Jacob comes into the land that will become Israel, pitching his tent and building an altar. It is a start.

— **The Rev. Brenda G. Husson**

Questions_____

Have you encountered the holy, but found that your past and your fear overshadow that experience?

Does your past make it hard to imagine a different future? Who might help you see differently?

Is there someone with whom you long to reconcile? How might you begin?

Prayer _____

Gracious God, when the past threatens to overwhelm me, let me expect and welcome the messengers you send to prepare me for a new future. Stop me, O Lord, when I become convinced that the measure I give must be the measure I shall get, and to trust that there is grace and abundant life enough for all. Thank you for the ever-present gift to grow in hope, faith, and love. *Amen.*

Genesis 34

34 Now Dinah the daughter of Leah, whom she had borne to Jacob, went out to visit the women of the region. ²When Shechem son of Hamor the Hivite, prince of the region, saw her, he seized her and lay with her by force. ³And his soul was drawn to Dinah daughter of Jacob; he loved the girl, and spoke tenderly to her. ⁴So Shechem spoke to his father Hamor, saying, "Get me this girl to be my wife." ⁵Now Jacob heard that Shechem had defiled his daughter Dinah; but his sons were with his cattle in the field, so Jacob held his peace until they came.

⁶And Hamor the father of Shechem went out to Jacob to speak with him, ⁷just as the sons of Jacob came in from the field. When they heard of it, the men were indignant and very angry, because he had committed an outrage in Israel by lying with Jacob's daughter, for such a thing ought not to be done. ⁸But Hamor spoke with them, saying, "The heart of my son Shechem longs for your daughter; please give her to him in marriage. ⁹Make marriages with us; give your daughters to us, and take our daughters for yourselves. ¹⁰You shall live with us; and the land shall be open to you; live and trade in it, and get property in it." ¹¹Shechem also said to her father and to her brothers, "Let me find favor with you, and whatever you say to me I will give. ¹²Put the marriage present and gift as high as you like, and I will give whatever you ask me; only give me the girl to be my wife." ¹³The sons of Jacob answered Shechem and his father Hamor deceitfully,

because he had defiled their sister Dinah. ¹⁴They said to them, "We cannot do this thing, to give our sister to one who is uncircumcised, for that would be a disgrace to us. ¹⁵Only on this condition will we consent to you: that you will become as we are and every male among you be circumcised. ¹⁶Then we will give our daughters to you, and we will take your daughters for ourselves, and we will live among you and become one people. ¹⁷But if you will not listen to us and be circumcised, then we will take our daughter and be gone."

¹⁸Their words pleased Hamor and Hamor's son Shechem. ¹⁹And the young man did not delay to do the thing, because he was delighted with Jacob's daughter. Now he was the most honored of all his family. ²⁰So Hamor and his son Shechem came to the gate of their city and spoke to the men of their city, saying, ²¹"These people are friendly with us; let them live in the land and trade in it, for the land is large enough for them; let us take their daughters in marriage, and let us give them our daughters. ²²Only on this condition will they agree to live among us, to become one people: that every male among us be circumcised as they are circumcised. ²³Will not their livestock, their property, and all their animals be ours? Only let us agree with them, and they will live among us." ²⁴And all who went out of the city gate heeded Hamor and his son Shechem; and every male was circumcised, all who went out of the gate of his city.

²⁵On the third day, when they were still in pain, two of the sons of Jacob, Simeon and Levi, Dinah's brothers, took their swords and came against the city unawares, and killed all the males. ²⁶They killed Hamor and his son Shechem with the sword, and took Dinah out

of Shechem's house, and went away. ²⁷And the other sons of Jacob came upon the slain, and plundered the city, because their sister had been defiled. ²⁸They took their flocks and their herds, their donkeys, and whatever was in the city and in the field. ²⁹All their wealth, all their little ones and their wives, all that was in the houses, they captured and made their prey. ³⁰Then Jacob said to Simeon and Levi, "You have brought trouble on me by making me odious to the inhabitants of the land, the Canaanites and the Perizzites; my numbers are few, and if they gather themselves against me and attack me, I shall be destroyed, both I and my household." ³¹But they said, "Should our sister be treated like a whore?"

Reflection

Ripped from the headlines? It feels that way. The Bible provides the whole story of the formation of the people of God, including parts we'd rather skip. Having crossed into Canaan with his household, Jacob now has a foothold in what will one day become the promised land. They are in Shechem (Nablus today).

All seems to be going well in this new land, until Jacob's daughter Dinah goes out to meet the local women. Finding her on her own, the son of the local ruler rapes her. Then he claims he loves her and wants to marry her. (This is a story both shocking and true to life. Even now, women who have been raped are sometimes required to marry the rapist. Further, we don't hear anymore from or about Dinah; she has become an object without voice or agency— another all too familiar reality today).

The man's father pleads with Jacob to allow his son to marry Dinah and pledges that the two peoples can become one community. Offering to fulfill any request, Dinah's brothers demand that all the men be circumcised, joining in the sign of the covenant made between God and Abraham, so the two peoples can indeed become one.

It is a ruse. The agreement is made; the men in the land are circumcised. While they are recovering, two of Jacob's sons kill all the men. Then the rest of the sons join in, plundering the city and taking *everything*, including women and children as well as goods and animals, as their own. Jacob speaks up, complaining that his family will no longer be welcome in the land. The brothers defend themselves, saying: Should he treat our sister as a harlot? Nice try.

Jacob's sons violate their relationship with God, using the sign of the covenant as a weapon of war. Jacob's concern is only for his personal safety. Dinah was raped, but she is abused again and again as she is used as an excuse for murder and revenge. God does not abandon us, but we surely abandon God.

— **The Rev. Brenda G. Husson**

Questions

Have you experienced a time when you realized your righteous indignation was just your own indignation? What did that feel like?

Have you ever experienced a time when you felt your experience or woundedness were co-opted for another's agenda? Were you able to speak up?

No one in this narrative speaks of a God of both judgment and mercy. In your own or your nation's history, have you witnessed one or two people or a movement relying upon God to effect righteousness?

Prayer

Dear Lord, when I take offense, help me to slow down and recognize my own agenda. When people are abused, let me come alongside them so that they may find their own words, their own voice, and their own way forward. Thank you, Lord Jesus, for bearing our wounds, our sins, and our sorrow that together we might rise with you into new life. *Amen.*

Genesis 35

35 God said to Jacob, "Arise, go up to Bethel, and settle there. Make an altar there to the God who appeared to you when you fled from your brother Esau." ²So Jacob said to his household and to all who were with him, "Put away the foreign gods that are among you, and purify yourselves, and change your clothes; ³then come, let us go up to Bethel, that I may make an altar there to the God who answered me in the day of my distress and has been with me wherever I have gone." ⁴So they gave to Jacob all the foreign gods that they had, and the rings that were in their ears; and Jacob hid them under the oak that was near Shechem. ⁵As they journeyed, a terror from God fell upon the cities all around them, so that no one pursued them.

⁶Jacob came to Luz (that is, Bethel), which is in the land of Canaan, he and all the people who were with him, ⁷and there he built an altar and called the place El-bethel, because it was there that God had revealed himself to him when he fled from his brother. ⁸And Deborah, Rebekah's nurse, died, and she was buried under an oak below Bethel. So it was called Allon-bacuth. ⁹God appeared to Jacob again when he came from Paddan-aram, and he blessed him. ¹⁰God said to him, "Your name is Jacob; no longer shall you be called Jacob, but Israel shall be your name." So he was called Israel. ¹¹God said to him, "I am God Almighty: be fruitful and multiply; a nation and a company of nations shall come from you, and kings shall spring from you. ¹²The land that I gave to Abraham and Isaac I

will give to you, and I will give the land to your offspring after you." ¹³Then God went up from him at the place where he had spoken with him. ¹⁴Jacob set up a pillar in the place where he had spoken with him, a pillar of stone; and he poured out a drink offering on it, and poured oil on it. ¹⁵So Jacob called the place where God had spoken with him Bethel.

¹⁶Then they journeyed from Bethel; and when they were still some distance from Ephrath, Rachel was in childbirth, and she had hard labor. ¹⁷When she was in her hard labor, the midwife said to her, "Do not be afraid; for now you will have another son." ¹⁸As her soul was departing (for she died), she named him Ben-oni; but his father called him Benjamin. ¹⁹So Rachel died, and she was buried on the way to Ephrath (that is, Bethlehem), ²⁰and Jacob set up a pillar at her grave; it is the pillar of Rachel's tomb, which is there to this day.

²¹Israel journeyed on, and pitched his tent beyond the tower of Eder. ²²While Israel lived in that land, Reuben went and lay with Bilhah his father's concubine; and Israel heard of it. Now the sons of Jacob were twelve. ²³The sons of Leah: Reuben (Jacob's firstborn), Simeon, Levi, Judah, Issachar, and Zebulun. ²⁴The sons of Rachel: Joseph and Benjamin. ²⁵The sons of Bilhah, Rachel's maid: Dan and Naphtali. ²⁶The sons of Zilpah, Leah's maid: Gad and Asher. These were the sons of Jacob who were born to him in Paddan-aram. ²⁷Jacob came to his father Isaac at Mamre, or Kiriath-arba (that is, Hebron), where Abraham and Isaac had resided as aliens. ²⁸Now the days of Isaac were one hundred eighty years. ²⁹And Isaac breathed his last; he died and was gathered to his people, old and full of days; and his sons Esau and Jacob buried him.

Reflection

So much has happened since Jacob first passed through Bethel. Since he first left home, Jacob has seen countless twists and turns and reversals of fortune. Life with Laban has given Jacob a taste of his own deceptive medicine. Building a family with Leah and Rachel has meant both heartache and love shared, struggles to conceive and the birth of many children. Jacob ran from Laban into a surprising reconciliation with Esau. Relationships have been built up and broken down, and so has Jacob himself.

Along the way, Jacob has set up pillars in the desert to mark these moments. He has put down tangible reminders of heavenly miracles and earthly covenants. Bethel was where that first began, when the stone he tried to use for a pillow supported a vision instead. God spoke to Jacob that night, and made him a promise: "Know that I am with you and will keep you wherever you go, and will bring you back to this land; for I will not leave you until I have done what I have promised you" (Genesis 28:15).

And even through all that has happened, God has kept that promise. God has never abandoned Jacob—and that has never been contingent on Jacob's own worthiness! When Jacob makes mistakes, God is there to point the way to a new future. When Jacob is wronged, God strengthens him to keep going. God hears the pleas of Rachel and Leah in the midst of a difficult marriage (to put it mildly).

In Genesis, we read the same truth and see it at work in our own lives. God does not promise us happiness, but God assures us of the divine presence. In return, God does not ask for our perfection but our faithfulness—our own attempt to be present to God's work in the world. From the beginning of creation to God's earthly incarnation, from numbering the stars with Abraham to the stone rolled away from the empty tomb, God has never promised us life would be easy. But God does promise that we will never be alone. And God asks us, in turn, to trust in our Creator.

— The Rev. Canon Eva Suarez

Questions

What are some of the pillars in your life? Are there moments you can look back on and see God's companionship on your own journey?

Jacob asks his family to cleanse themselves, not just of ill-gotten gains from the city of Shechem but also of the household gods Rachel has kept from her homeland. Not every piece of our past can come with us into new life. Are there habits, interests, or relationships you've had to let go of in order to follow Jesus?

Prayer

Gracious and loving God, thank you for bringing us to this day. Please draw near to us and guide us where you would have us go. Help us to see your Holy Spirit at work in the world and strengthen us to follow you. We ask all this in the name of your Son our Savior, Jesus Christ. *Amen.*

Genesis 36

36 These are the descendants of Esau (that is, Edom). ²Esau took his wives from the Canaanites: Adah daughter of Elon the Hittite, Oholibamah daughter of Anah son of Zibeon the Hivite, ³and Basemath, Ishmael's daughter, sister of Nebaioth. ⁴Adah bore Eliphaz to Esau; Basemath bore Reuel; ⁵and Oholibamah bore Jeush, Jalam, and Korah. These are the sons of Esau who were born to him in the land of Canaan. ⁶Then Esau took his wives, his sons, his daughters, and all the members of his household, his cattle, all his livestock, and all the property he had acquired in the land of Canaan; and he moved to a land some distance from his brother Jacob. ⁷For their possessions were too great for them to live together; the land where they were staying could not support them because of their livestock. ⁸So Esau settled in the hill country of Seir; Esau is Edom.

⁹These are the descendants of Esau, ancestor of the Edomites, in the hill country of Seir. ¹⁰These are the names of Esau's sons: Eliphaz son of Adah the wife of Esau; Reuel, the son of Esau's wife Basemath. ¹¹The sons of Eliphaz were Teman, Omar, Zepho, Gatam, and Kenaz. ¹²(Timna was a concubine of Eliphaz, Esau's son; she bore Amalek to Eliphaz.) These were the sons of Adah, Esau's wife. ¹³These were the sons of Reuel: Nahath, Zerah, Shammah, and Mizzah. These were the sons of Esau's wife, Basemath. ¹⁴These were the sons of Esau's wife Oholibamah, daughter of Anah son of Zibeon: she bore to Esau Jeush, Jalam, and Korah.

¹⁵These are the clans of the sons of Esau. The sons of Eliphaz the firstborn of Esau: the clans Teman, Omar, Zepho, Kenaz, ¹⁶Korah, Gatam, and Amalek; these are the clans of Eliphaz in the land of Edom; they are the sons of Adah. ¹⁷These are the sons of Esau's son Reuel: the clans Nahath, Zerah, Shammah, and Mizzah; these are the clans of Reuel in the land of Edom; they are the sons of Esau's wife Basemath. ¹⁸These are the sons of Esau's wife Oholibamah: the clans Jeush, Jalam, and Korah; these are the clans born of Esau's wife Oholibamah, the daughter of Anah. ¹⁹These are the sons of Esau (that is, Edom), and these are their clans.

²⁰These are the sons of Seir the Horite, the inhabitants of the land: Lotan, Shobal, Zibeon, Anah, ²¹Dishon, Ezer, and Dishan; these are the clans of the Horites, the sons of Seir in the land of Edom. ²²The sons of Lotan were Hori and Heman; and Lotan's sister was Timna. ²³These are the sons of Shobal: Alvan, Manahath, Ebal, Shepho, and Onam. ²⁴These are the sons of Zibeon: Aiah and Anah; he is the Anah who found the springs in the wilderness, as he pastured the donkeys of his father Zibeon. ²⁵These are the children of Anah: Dishon and Oholibamah daughter of Anah. ²⁶These are the sons of Dishon: Hemdan, Eshban, Ithran, and Cheran. ²⁷These are the sons of Ezer: Bilhan, Zaavan, and Akan. ²⁸These are the sons of Dishan: Uz and Aran. ²⁹These are the clans of the Horites: the clans Lotan, Shobal, Zibeon, Anah, ³⁰Dishon, Ezer, and Dishan; these are the clans of the Horites, clan by clan in the land of Seir.

³¹These are the kings who reigned in the land of Edom, before any king reigned over the Israelites. ³²Bela son of Beor reigned in Edom, the name of his city being Dinhabah. ³³Bela

died, and Jobab son of Zerah of Bozrah succeeded him as king. ³⁴Jobab died, and Husham of the land of the Temanites succeeded him as king. ³⁵Husham died, and Hadad son of Bedad, who defeated Midian in the country of Moab, succeeded him as king, the name of his city being Avith. ³⁶Hadad died, and Samlah of Masrekah succeeded him as king. ³⁷Samlah died, and Shaul of Rehoboth on the Euphrates succeeded him as king. ³⁸Shaul died, and Baal-hanan son of Achbor succeeded him as king. ³⁹Baal-hanan son of Achbor died, and Hadar succeeded him as king, the name of his city being Pau; his wife's name was Mehetabel, the daughter of Matred, daughter of Me-zahab. ⁴⁰These are the names of the clans of Esau, according to their families and their localities by their names: the clans Timna, Alvah, Jetheth, ⁴¹Oholibamah, Elah, Pinon, ⁴²Kenaz, Teman, Mibzar, ⁴³Magdiel, and Iram; these are the clans of Edom (that is, Esau, the father of Edom), according to their settlements in the land that they held.

Reflection

Congratulations! You made it through the thirty-sixth chapter of Genesis. Here we return to Esau's journey and his family. This chapter feels like the kind of biblical narrative some people love to lampoon; how so-and-so begat so-and-so, and so on and so on. Ancient audiences appreciated genealogies, and recounting the generations was a way to trace historical and cultural shifts. Before we write sections like this off as a matter of taste, consider the current popularity of ancestry websites and genetic testing. A lot of us want to know where we come from.

Yet unlike other genealogies from scripture, this isn't a chunk of "our" family tree: the Edomites were enemies of the Israelites throughout history. This passage comes at a turning point in our narrative, as we shift our focus from the story of Jacob to the story of his sons. Earlier in Genesis, as the focus shifts from Abraham's story to Isaac's, we are told the genealogy of Ishmael. It is almost as if our authors do not want us to forget the less fortunate son, the older brothers who do not share in God's covenant with Abraham.

Esau is a poignant figure. A moment of shortsightedness as a young man in competition with his brother has tremendous repercussions. Relinquishing his birthright quickly becomes the loss of his father's blessing. Yet somehow, Esau finds a way to carry on and build a life. I bet many of us can remember a moment of poor judgment that reverberated more harshly than we thought possible. Though Esau's life and lineage are not our focus, the "family resemblance" is clear.

We can still learn something from our distant cousins, Esau and Ishmael. First, life goes on. Even after our most painful disappointments, when we cannot imagine what comes next, God has promised us a future. Second, we can learn from their experiences of hurt and rejection how not to be people that hurt and reject others. Our story is our story, but in our lives today, as we strive to be the body of Christ, we have to help all our siblings to have a future.

— The Rev. Canon Eva Suarez

Questions _____

Take a look at your own family tree. Are there mysterious branches, or people with whom you have lost touch? Spend some time learning and reflecting on your own story.

How can you apply the lessons offered by Esau and Ishmael to your own life?

Prayer _____

Most merciful God, we thank you for our creation, preservation, and all the blessings of this life. Please continue to cover us with your grace and love and help us to share that love with others. Please help us to grow in love and knowledge of you, and to live as your children, for the sake of your son our Savior, Jesus Christ. *Amen*.

Genesis 37

37 Jacob settled in the land where his father had lived as an alien, the land of Canaan. ²This is the story of the family of Jacob. Joseph, being seventeen years old, was shepherding the flock with his brothers; he was a helper to the sons of Bilhah and Zilpah, his father's wives; and Joseph brought a bad report of them to their father. ³Now Israel loved Joseph more than any other of his children, because he was the son of his old age; and he had made him a long robe with sleeves. ⁴But when his brothers saw that their father loved him more than all his brothers, they hated him, and could not speak peaceably to him.

⁵Once Joseph had a dream, and when he told it to his brothers, they hated him even more. ⁶He said to them, "Listen to this dream that I dreamed. ⁷There we were, binding sheaves in the field. Suddenly my sheaf rose and stood upright; then your sheaves gathered around it, and bowed down to my sheaf." ⁸His brothers said to him, "Are you indeed to reign over us? Are you indeed to have dominion over us?" So they hated him even more because of his dreams and his words. ⁹He had another dream, and told it to his brothers, saying, "Look, I have had another dream: the sun, the moon, and eleven stars were bowing down to me." ¹⁰But when he told it to his father and to his brothers, his father rebuked him, and said to him, "What kind of dream is this that you have had? Shall we indeed come, I and your mother and your brothers, and bow to the ground before you?" ¹¹So his

brothers were jealous of him, but his father kept the matter in mind.

¹²Now his brothers went to pasture their father's flock near Shechem. ¹³And Israel said to Joseph, "Are not your brothers pasturing the flock at Shechem? Come, I will send you to them." He answered, "Here I am." ¹⁴So he said to him, "Go now, see if it is well with your brothers and with the flock; and bring word back to me." So he sent him from the valley of Hebron. He came to Shechem, ¹⁵and a man found him wandering in the fields; the man asked him, "What are you seeking?" ¹⁶"I am seeking my brothers," he said; "tell me, please, where they are pasturing the flock." ¹⁷The man said, "They have gone away, for I heard them say, 'Let us go to Dothan.'" So Joseph went after his brothers, and found them at Dothan. ¹⁸They saw him from a distance, and before he came near to them, they conspired

to kill him. ¹⁹They said to one another, "Here comes this dreamer. ²⁰Come now, let us kill him and throw him into one of the pits; then we shall say that a wild animal has devoured him, and we shall see what will become of his dreams." ²¹But when Reuben heard it, he delivered him out of their hands, saying, "Let us not take his life." ²²Reuben said to them, "Shed no blood; throw him into this pit here in the wilderness, but lay no hand on him" — that he might rescue him out of their hand and restore him to his father.

²³So when Joseph came to his brothers, they stripped him of his robe, the long robe with sleeves that he wore; ²⁴and they took him and threw him into a pit. The pit was empty; there was no water in it. ²⁵Then they sat down to eat; and looking up they saw a caravan of Ishmaelites coming from Gilead, with their camels carrying gum, balm, and

resin, on their way to carry it down to Egypt. ²⁶Then Judah said to his brothers, "What profit is it if we kill our brother and conceal his blood? ²⁷Come, let us sell him to the Ishmaelites, and not lay our hands on him, for he is our brother, our own flesh." And his brothers agreed. ²⁸When some Midianite traders passed by, they drew Joseph up, lifting him out of the pit, and sold him to the Ishmaelites for twenty pieces of silver. And they took Joseph to Egypt. ²⁹When Reuben returned to the pit and saw that Joseph was not in the pit, he tore his clothes. ³⁰He returned to his brothers, and said, "The boy is gone; and I, where can I turn?"

³¹Then they took Joseph's robe, slaughtered a goat, and dipped the robe in the blood. ³²They had the long robe with sleeves taken to their father, and they said, "This we have found; see now whether it is your son's robe or not." ³³He recognized it, and said, "It is my son's robe! A wild animal has devoured him; Joseph is without doubt torn to pieces." ³⁴Then Jacob tore his garments, and put sackcloth on his loins, and mourned for his son many days. ³⁵All his sons and all his daughters sought to comfort him; but he refused to be comforted, and said, "No, I shall go down to Sheol to my son, mourning." Thus his father bewailed him. ³⁶Meanwhile the Midianites had sold him in Egypt to Potiphar, one of Pharaoh's officials, the captain of the guard.

Reflection

"So they hated him even more because of his dreams and his words."

The searing hatred of Joseph's brothers still singes the pages of scripture thousands of years later. The sons of Jacob hate their brother because he is a tattletale who "brings a bad report" on them to their father. They hate their brother because Jacob dotes on him and loves him more than all the rest of his children. They hate their brother because their father makes for Joseph a coat of many colors—an outward and visible sign of his undisputed status as Jacob's favorite son.

But most of all, they hate their brother for his dreams. Joseph's night visions clearly foretell his own future exultation and his family's humbling. A teenager dreaming that his older brothers—and even his father!—would one day bow down in obeisance before him? Such portents would have scandalized the people of Joseph's profoundly patriarchal culture. And Joseph's brothers hate him "yet the more" because of his dreams.

Though centuries separate us from the sibling rivalry of these ancient brothers, the seething hatred that drives them to the brink of fratricide is still, sadly, familiar. We live in a world still riven and ruined by hatred: hatred within our homes, our families, our communities, our nations, and our own hearts. We find in ourselves the same bitterness and brokenness felt by Joseph's brothers, even if we've never robbed a relative of a rich coat and thrown them into a ditch. We know the power of hatred because it has been wielded against us, and we have harbored it within our own souls.

But the promise of this story—the promise of all of scripture—is that God's power is never stopped or stymied by fierce human hatred. Indeed, God's power works through the hatred we feel and the hurt we cause to bring forth better things than we can ask for or imagine. We see that as Joseph's saga unfolds. And we see that most perfectly when Christ Jesus transforms the hateful symbol of the cross into the source of our hope and joy.

— The Very Rev. Dane E. Boston

Questions _____

When have you grappled with feelings of intense anger and hatred in your life?

How might you yield up even the bitter and broken corners of your heart to God's redeeming grace?

Prayer _____

Lord Jesus our savior and our brother, you gave your back to the smiters and your cheeks to those who plucked off the hair, and you hid not your face from shame and spitting. You bore for us the weight of human sin and the brunt of human hatred. By the grace of your Holy Spirit, take away the hate that divides nation against nation and heart against heart and make us all sisters and brothers of your Heavenly Father, with whom you live and reign with that same Spirit, ever one God. *Amen.*

Genesis 38

38 It happened at that time that Judah went down from his brothers and settled near a certain Adullamite whose name was Hirah. ²There Judah saw the daughter of a certain Canaanite whose name was Shua; he married her and went in to her. ³She conceived and bore a son; and he named him Er. ⁴Again she conceived and bore a son whom she named Onan. ⁵Yet again she bore a son, and she named him Shelah. She was in Chezib when she bore him. ⁶Judah took a wife for Er his firstborn; her name was Tamar. ⁷But Er, Judah's firstborn, was wicked in the sight of the Lord, and the Lord put him to death. ⁸Then Judah said to Onan, "Go in to your brother's wife and perform the duty of a brother-in-law to her; raise up offspring for your brother." ⁹But since Onan knew that the offspring would not be his, he spilled his semen on the ground whenever he went in to his brother's wife, so that he would not give offspring to his brother. ¹⁰What he did was displeasing in the sight of the Lord, and he put him to death also. ¹¹Then Judah said to his daughter-in-law Tamar, "Remain a widow in your father's house until my son Shelah grows up" —for he feared that he too would die, like his brothers. So Tamar went to live in her father's house.

¹²In course of time the wife of Judah, Shua's daughter, died; when Judah's time of mourning was over, he went up to Timnah to his sheepshearers, he and his friend Hirah the Adullamite. ¹³When Tamar was told, "Your father-in-law is going up to Timnah to shear his sheep," ¹⁴she put off her widow's garments,

put on a veil, wrapped herself up, and sat down at the entrance to Enaim, which is on the road to Timnah. She saw that Shelah was grown up, yet she had not been given to him in marriage. ¹⁵When Judah saw her, he thought her to be a prostitute, for she had covered her face. ¹⁶He went over to her at the road side, and said, "Come, let me come in to you," for he did not know that she was his daughter-in-law. She said, "What will you give me, that you may come in to me?" ¹⁷He answered, "I will send you a kid from the flock." And she said, "Only if you give me a pledge, until you send it." ¹⁸He said, "What pledge shall I give you?" She replied, "Your signet and your cord, and the staff that is in your hand." So he gave them to her, and went in to her, and she conceived by him. ¹⁹Then she got up and went away, and taking off her veil she put on the garments of her widowhood. ²⁰When Judah sent the kid by his friend

the Adullamite, to recover the pledge from the woman, he could not find her. ²¹He asked the townspeople, "Where is the temple prostitute who was at Enaim by the wayside?" But they said, "No prostitute has been here." ²²So he returned to Judah, and said, "I have not found her; moreover the townspeople said, 'No prostitute has been here.'" ²³Judah replied, "Let her keep the things as her own, otherwise we will be laughed at; you see, I sent this kid, and you could not find her."

²⁴About three months later Judah was told, "Your daughter-in-law Tamar has played the whore; moreover she is pregnant as a result of whoredom." And Judah said, "Bring her out, and let her be burned." ²⁵As she was being brought out, she sent word to her father-in-law, "It was the owner of these who made me pregnant." And she said, "Take note, please, whose these are, the signet and the cord and the staff." ²⁶Then

Judah acknowledged them and said, "She is more in the right than I, since I did not give her to my son Shelah." And he did not lie with her again. ²⁷When the time of her delivery came, there were twins in her womb. ²⁸While she was in labor, one put out a hand; and the midwife took and bound on his hand a crimson thread, saying, "This one came out first." ²⁹But just then he drew back his hand, and out came his brother; and she said, "What a breach you have made for yourself!" Therefore he was named Perez. ³⁰Afterward his brother came out with the crimson thread on his hand; and he was named Zerah.

Reflection

There are no minor characters in God's story. Few chapters of scripture teach this truth as powerfully as Genesis 38.

But before we can learn *from* Tamar's story, we must learn *about* it. A woman's identity in the ancient world was established through her relationship to three men: her father, her husband, and her son. At marriage, a woman left her father's care and became part of her husband's house. If she were widowed, her hope for the future would be set on the sons her late husband had given her.

But what if a woman's husband died childless? "Levirate marriage" solved this significant problem. The brother of the deceased married his widow and "raised up seed" to his dead brother. Thus, the family line continued, and widows were saved from utter abandonment in a patriarchal world.

Understanding this background helps us understand Tamar's story. Having lost two childless husbands in rapid succession, her status is tenuous. Judah's unwillingness to give her to his third son in marriage—an unwillingness founded in his unfair suspicion of Tamar after the deaths of his first two wicked sons—dooms her to an uncertain future: living as a widow in her own father's house, still bound to the family of her dead husbands. So, Tamar takes matters into her own hands and secures her own future and the future of Judah's line by deceiving and seducing her father-in-law.

Surely Tamar's tenacity and single-minded pursuit of what she knows to be right warrant our admiration, even if we stop short of emulating her actions. But there is more. Though her story is told here in just 30 brief verses, this is not the last time Tamar is mentioned in the Bible. We find her name invoked in the blessing bestowed on the union of Boaz and the faithful Gentile Ruth, a union that leads directly to King David. And we find her, at last, named in the genealogy of Jesus Christ given in Matthew 1.

There are no minor characters in the story of God's redemption. This is true for Tamar, and it is true for us.

— The Very Rev. Dane E. Boston

Questions

Can you identify people who, though they may seem like "minor characters," have played a major role in your life and faith?

What deep truths will you cling to tenaciously, even when all around you deny them?

Prayer

O God of the widow and the orphan, the lowly and the least, the forgotten people and the minor characters of this world: help us to see the dignity of your image in every human being and let us never forget that you come to us not as we should be or as we wish we were, but as we truly are, through Jesus Christ our Lord. *Amen.*

Genesis 39

39 Now Joseph was taken down to Egypt, and Potiphar, an officer of Pharaoh, the captain of the guard, an Egyptian, bought him from the Ishmaelites who had brought him down there. ²The LORD was with Joseph, and he became a successful man; he was in the house of his Egyptian master. ³His master saw that the LORD was with him, and that the LORD caused all that he did to prosper in his hands. ⁴So Joseph found favor in his sight and attended him; he made him overseer of his house and put him in charge of all that he had. ⁵From the time that he made him overseer in his house and over all that he had, the LORD blessed the Egyptian's house for Joseph's sake; the blessing of the LORD was on all that he had, in house and field. ⁶So he left all that he had in Joseph's charge; and, with him there, he had no concern for anything but the food that he ate. Now Joseph was handsome and good-looking.

⁷And after a time his master's wife cast her eyes on Joseph and said, "Lie with me." ⁸But he refused and said to his master's wife, "Look, with me here, my master has no concern about anything in the house, and he has put everything that he has in my hand. ⁹He is not greater in this house than I am, nor has he kept back anything from me except yourself, because you are his wife. How then could I do this great wickedness, and sin against God?" ¹⁰And although she spoke to Joseph day after day, he would not consent to lie beside her or to be with her.

[11]One day, however, when he went into the house to do his work, and while no one else was in the house, [12]she caught hold of his garment, saying, "Lie with me!" But he left his garment in her hand, and fled and ran outside.

[13]When she saw that he had left his garment in her hand and had fled outside, [14]she called out to the members of her household and said to them, "See, my husband has brought among us a Hebrew to insult us! He came in to me to lie with me, and I cried out with a loud voice; [15]and when he heard me raise my voice and cry out, he left his garment beside me, and fled outside." [16]Then she kept his garment by her until his master came home, [17]and she told him the same story, saying, "The Hebrew servant, whom you have brought among us, came in to me to insult me; [18]but as soon as I raised my voice and cried out, he left his garment beside me, and fled outside."

[19]When his master heard the words that his wife spoke to him, saying, "This is the way your servant treated me," he became enraged. [20]And Joseph's master took him and put him into the prison, the place where the king's prisoners were confined; he remained there in prison. [21]But the LORD was with Joseph and showed him steadfast love; he gave him favor in the sight of the chief jailer. [22]The chief jailer committed to Joseph's care all the prisoners who were in the prison, and whatever was done there, he was the one who did it. [23]The chief jailer paid no heed to anything that was in Joseph's care, because the LORD was with him; and whatever he did, the LORD made it prosper.

Reflection

Joseph has been promoted to serve as the most trusted overseer in Potiphar's household. He moves about, makes decisions, and manages the inner sanctum of his earthly master. Unfortunately for him, though, his attractive appearance, daily on view and in close proximity to the mistress of the house, catches her lustful eye. Potiphar's wife sets her sights on seducing him. With relentless sexual advances, she pursues him, tempting him without mercy and wielding her power to exploit.

But Joseph resists and refuses to succumb. He draws on the strength of his Lord in the face of temptation and clings to his inner sense of righteousness: right action, right thought, and right relationship. Yet, even in a dramatic, last-ditch effort to flee the scene of temptation, the situation conspires against him. He is falsely accused and goes to prison a blameless man to the end.

His prison term, nevertheless, becomes one more opportunity to minister in God's name. The chief jailer trusts him and commits the prisoners to his spiritual care. Even from his jail cell, God uses Joseph, and his righteousness shines forth.

The colorful character of Potiphar's wife shows up in the sacred writings of all three of the Abrahamic faiths—Christianity, Judaism, and Islam—underscoring the power, relatability, and indelibility of the imagery and themes of this story. Interestingly in the Quran, a test is employed to determine Joseph's guilt or innocence. According to the test, if the cloak rips from the front, Joseph is a liar; if from the back, he tells the truth. The story, as told in the book of Genesis, however, makes no such determination of culpability, emphasizing that God's mercy and grace are bestowed upon guilty and innocent alike. This sentiment is echoed in Romans 5:8—"While we still were sinners Christ died for us"—demonstrating that divine love is wholly undeserved and given first and foremost as gift, regardless of our fitness or merit.

— The Rev. Christine Trainor

Questions _____

An adage encourages one to keep their friends close and their enemies closer. Potiphar believes that he has been betrayed by his most trusted servant. Have you been in a situation where you felt betrayed by someone you trusted? How did you reconcile this betrayal?

Potiphar's wife seems intent on entrapping Joseph and exploiting her power over him. Have you had to navigate such a situation? How did you find an "inner compass" in such a situation?

Joseph goes to jail blameless much as Jesus was crucified blameless between two criminals. What parallels do you see in these two accounts?

Prayer _____

O God, our Protector, deliver us from those who would wish us harm. Help us to think and do only those things that are righteous in your sight. Where we have wronged others, may we make amends. Where we have been wronged, may we respond in the way of your grace and mercy. Draw us ever closer to you in care and service in Jesus's name. *Amen.*

Genesis 40

40 Some time after this, the cupbearer of the king of Egypt and his baker offended their lord the king of Egypt. [2]Pharaoh was angry with his two officers, the chief cupbearer and the chief baker, [3]and he put them in custody in the house of the captain of the guard, in the prison where Joseph was confined. [4]The captain of the guard charged Joseph with them, and he waited on them; and they continued for some time in custody.

[5]One night they both dreamed—the cupbearer and the baker of the king of Egypt, who were confined in the prison—each his own dream, and each dream with its own meaning. [6]When Joseph came to them in the morning, he saw that they were troubled. [7]So he asked Pharaoh's officers, who were with him in custody in his master's house, "Why are your faces downcast today?" [8]They said to him, "We have had dreams, and there is no one to interpret them." And Joseph said to them, "Do not interpretations belong to God? Please tell them to me." [9]So the chief cupbearer told his dream to Joseph, and said to him, "In my dream there was a vine before me, [10]and on the vine there were three branches. As soon as it budded, its blossoms came out and the clusters ripened into grapes. [11]Pharaoh's cup was in my hand; and I took the grapes and pressed them into Pharaoh's cup, and placed the cup in Pharaoh's hand." [12]Then Joseph said to him, "This is its interpretation: the three branches are three days; [13]within three days Pharaoh will lift up your head and restore

you to your office; and you shall place Pharaoh's cup in his hand, just as you used to do when you were his cupbearer. ¹⁴But remember me when it is well with you; please do me the kindness to make mention of me to Pharaoh, and so get me out of this place. ¹⁵For in fact I was stolen out of the land of the Hebrews; and here also I have done nothing that they should have put me into the dungeon." ¹⁶When the chief baker saw that the interpretation was favorable, he said to Joseph, "I also had a dream: there were three cake baskets on my head, ¹⁷and in the uppermost basket there were all sorts of baked food for Pharaoh, but the birds were eating it out of the basket on my head." ¹⁸And

Joseph answered, "This is its interpretation: the three baskets are three days; ¹⁹within three days Pharaoh will lift up your head—from you! —and hang you on a pole; and the birds will eat the flesh from you."

²⁰On the third day, which was Pharaoh's birthday, he made a feast for all his servants, and lifted up the head of the chief cupbearer and the head of the chief baker among his servants. ²¹He restored the chief cupbearer to his cupbearing, and he placed the cup in Pharaoh's hand; ²²but the chief baker he hanged, just as Joseph had interpreted to them. ²³Yet the chief cupbearer did not remember Joseph, but forgot him.

Reflection

When Joseph hears that the baker and cupbearer have had dreams in prison for which the meaning is sought, he asks, "Do not interpretations belong to God?"

This story takes dreams seriously and resonates with other places in Holy Scripture that refer to dreams. For example, Joseph's forebear Jacob lays his head upon a stone in the wilderness, falls into a deep sleep, and dreams about a mystical ladder that bridges the divide between heaven and earth. Angels ascend and descend this ladder, shuttling back and forth freely between the two realms of heaven and earth. Jacob had this dream in a place called Beth-El, which means "house of God." The dream becomes a defining moment in his faith journey, in his taking his place as a patriarch of the Israelites, and in his deepening trust that he will help bring forth a great nation in which God's will shall be done on earth as it is in heaven.

It is interesting to note that this important and constituting vision comes in a dream, because of course, that is often how God's Word comes to people of faith. Think about it: we spend about a third of our lives sleeping. If we agree that God is always working in our lives, it makes sense that God works in our sleeping as well as our waking. Many of us may be even more open to God's Word when we are sleeping, when our subconscious lays bare, when our minds are more susceptible to suggestion.

The emphasis on dreams in the Bible encourages us to think about the ways in which God's Word comes to us. Why would it not come in sleep and imagination, places where our mind opens itself to play, creativity, the subconscious, and the sublime?

— **The Rev. Christine Trainor**

Questions

What do you think about the Word of God coming to us in sleep and imagination?

The church has historically been a patron and supporter of the arts but has also harbored suspicion and anxiety about artists and their proclivity to challenge or subvert the status quo. What do you think about the relationship between your faith and artistic expression?

Prayer

O Creator God, each moment holds the potential of new possibility. Sometimes it can be hard to see the way forward or the way through. Help me to trust that the divine force of creativity ever brings new life, that God's dreams are being fulfilled, and that something new is ever waiting to be born. I pray in the name of your Word revealed since the foundations of the world. *Amen.*

Genesis 41

41 After two whole years, Pharaoh dreamed that he was standing by the Nile, [2]and there came up out of the Nile seven sleek and fat cows, and they grazed in the reed grass. [3]Then seven other cows, ugly and thin, came up out of the Nile after them, and stood by the other cows on the bank of the Nile. [4]The ugly and thin cows ate up the seven sleek and fat cows. And Pharaoh awoke. [5]Then he fell asleep and dreamed a second time; seven ears of grain, plump and good, were growing on one stalk. [6]Then seven ears, thin and blighted by the east wind, sprouted after them. [7]The thin ears swallowed up the seven plump and full ears. Pharaoh awoke, and it was a dream. [8]In the morning his spirit was troubled; so he sent and called for all the magicians of Egypt and all its wise men. Pharaoh told them his dreams, but there was no one who could interpret them to Pharaoh.

[9]Then the chief cupbearer said to Pharaoh, "I remember my faults today. [10]Once Pharaoh was angry with his servants, and put me and the chief baker in custody in the house of the captain of the guard. [11]We dreamed on the same night, he and I, each having a dream with its own meaning. [12]A young Hebrew was there with us, a servant of the captain of the guard. When we told him, he interpreted our dreams to us, giving an interpretation to each according to his dream. [13]As he interpreted to us, so it turned out; I was restored to my office, and the baker was hanged." [14]Then Pharaoh sent for Joseph, and he was hurriedly brought

out of the dungeon. When he had shaved himself and changed his clothes, he came in before Pharaoh. ¹⁵And Pharaoh said to Joseph, "I have had a dream, and there is no one who can interpret it. I have heard it said of you that when you hear a dream you can interpret it." ¹⁶Joseph answered Pharaoh, "It is not I; God will give Pharaoh a favorable answer."

¹⁷Then Pharaoh said to Joseph, "In my dream I was standing on the banks of the Nile; ¹⁸and seven cows, fat and sleek, came up out of the Nile and fed in the reed grass. ¹⁹Then seven other cows came up after them, poor, very ugly, and thin. Never had I seen such ugly ones in all the land of Egypt. ²⁰The thin and ugly cows ate up the first seven fat cows, ²¹but when they had eaten them no one would have known that they had done so, for they were still as ugly as before. Then I awoke. ²²I fell asleep a second time and I saw in my dream seven ears of grain, full and good, growing on one stalk, ²³and seven ears, withered, thin, and blighted by the east wind, sprouting after them; ²⁴and the thin ears swallowed up the seven good ears. But when I told it to the magicians, there was no one who could explain it to me."

²⁵Then Joseph said to Pharaoh, "Pharaoh's dreams are one and the same; God has revealed to Pharaoh what he is about to do. ²⁶The seven good cows are seven years, and the seven good ears are seven years; the dreams are one. ²⁷The seven lean and ugly cows that came up after them are seven years, as are the seven empty ears blighted by the east wind. They are seven years of famine. ²⁸It is as I told Pharaoh; God has shown to Pharaoh what he is about to do. ²⁹There will come seven years of great plenty throughout all the land of Egypt. ³⁰After them there will arise seven years of famine, and all the plenty will be forgotten in the land of Egypt; the famine will consume the land. ³¹The

plenty will no longer be known in the land because of the famine that will follow, for it will be very grievous. [32]And the doubling of Pharaoh's dream means that the thing is fixed by God, and God will shortly bring it about.

[33]Now therefore let Pharaoh select a man who is discerning and wise, and set him over the land of Egypt. [34]Let Pharaoh proceed to appoint overseers over the land, and take one-fifth of the produce of the land of Egypt during the seven plenteous years. [35]Let them gather all the food of these good years that are coming, and lay up grain under the authority of Pharaoh for food in the cities, and let them keep it. [36]That food shall be a reserve for the land against the seven years of famine that are to befall the land of Egypt, so that the land may not perish through the famine." [37]The proposal pleased Pharaoh and all his servants. [38]Pharaoh said to his servants,

"Can we find anyone else like this—one in whom is the spirit of God?" [39]So Pharaoh said to Joseph, "Since God has shown you all this, there is no one so discerning and wise as you. [40]You shall be over my house, and all my people shall order themselves as you command; only with regard to the throne will I be greater than you." [41]And Pharaoh said to Joseph, "See, I have set you over all the land of Egypt." [42]Removing his signet ring from his hand, Pharaoh put it on Joseph's hand; he arrayed him in garments of fine linen, and put a gold chain around his neck. [43]He had him ride in the chariot of his second-in-command; and they cried out in front of him, "Bow the knee!" Thus he set him over all the land of Egypt. [44]Moreover Pharaoh said to Joseph, "I am Pharaoh, and without your consent no one shall lift up hand or foot in all the land of Egypt." [45]Pharaoh gave Joseph the name Zaphenath-paneah;

and he gave him Asenath daughter of Potiphera, priest of On, as his wife. Thus Joseph gained authority over the land of Egypt.

46Joseph was thirty years old when he entered the service of Pharaoh king of Egypt. And Joseph went out from the presence of Pharaoh, and went through all the land of Egypt. 47During the seven plenteous years the earth produced abundantly. 48He gathered up all the food of the seven years when there was plenty in the land of Egypt, and stored up food in the cities; he stored up in every city the food from the fields around it. 49So Joseph stored up grain in such abundance—like the sand of the sea—that he stopped measuring it; it was beyond measure. 50Before the years of famine came, Joseph had two sons, whom Asenath daughter of Potiphera, priest of On, bore to him. 51Joseph named the firstborn Manasseh, "For," he said, "God has made me forget all my hardship and all my father's house." 52The second he named Ephraim, "For God has made me fruitful in the land of my misfortunes." 53The seven years of plenty that prevailed in the land of Egypt came to an end; 54and the seven years of famine began to come, just as Joseph had said. There was famine in every country, but throughout the land of Egypt there was bread. 55When all the land of Egypt was famished, the people cried to Pharaoh for bread. Pharaoh said to all the Egyptians, "Go to Joseph; what he says to you, do." 56And since the famine had spread over all the land, Joseph opened all the storehouses, and sold to the Egyptians, for the famine was severe in the land of Egypt. 57Moreover, all the world came to Joseph in Egypt to buy grain, because the famine became severe throughout the world.

Reflection

God gives us exactly what we need in order to do the work God needs us to do.

This is hard for many of us to believe. We ask, "Who me?" We argue, "But I'm just a ____," and we fill in the blank with some self-deprecative statement questioning what we could possibly offer to be helpful to bear for the sake of the gospel. Or we believe that in order for us to be of any use to God, some grand intervention of the Holy Spirit would need to occur, changing us into someone new, bestowing on us some gift we do not currently possess.

Who knows how many dreams Joseph interpreted in his young life? How often had his interpretations gone unheard or ignored? How many dreams had the brothers had to endure Joseph explain before they had enough and threw him into the pit?

In prison, Joseph simply does what he is good at; he interprets dreams. There is no instant reward for Joseph being Joseph. After the dreams are interpreted, Joseph is still in prison. He is still Joseph. But when the interpretation of dreams is what is needed, it is Joseph whom they seek. And his seemingly simple gift of giving meaning to dreams saves countless lives.

God makes us who we are and bestows upon us the gifts God needs us to possess in order to be who it is God made us each to be. All God asks is that we keep offering our gifts, even if they appear to go unappreciated, make little difference in the grand scheme of things, or get us thrown into a pit. Someday, God will need us to offer the gifts God gave us, and in that moment, all we need do is say yes.

— The Rt. Rev. Jeffrey W. Mello

Questions _____

What gift(s) has God given you? Can you make a list and offer God thanks for your gifts?

When the Pharaoh needed someone to interpret his dreams, it was the chief cupbearer who told Pharoah about Joseph and his gift of interpretation. Think of those you know and love, perhaps those with whom you work or share in ministry. Can you think of a gift each one of them might possess, even if they might not see it in themselves?

Prayer _____

Gracious God, giver of every good gift. We thank you for bestowing in us plentiful gifts we need to, with your help, be the people you call us to be. Give us wisdom to know our gifts, courage to share them, and the grace to see the gifts of others that we might, when the time comes, use our gifts to your purposes and to the honor and glory of your name. *Amen.*

Genesis 42

42 When Jacob learned that there was grain in Egypt, he said to his sons, "Why do you keep looking at one another? ²I have heard," he said, "that there is grain in Egypt; go down and buy grain for us there, that we may live and not die." ³So ten of Joseph's brothers went down to buy grain in Egypt. ⁴But Jacob did not send Joseph's brother Benjamin with his brothers, for he feared that harm might come to him. ⁵Thus the sons of Israel were among the other people who came to buy grain, for the famine had reached the land of Canaan. ⁶Now Joseph was governor over the land; it was he who sold to all the people of the land. And Joseph's brothers came and bowed themselves before him with their faces to the ground.

⁷When Joseph saw his brothers, he recognized them, but he treated them like strangers and spoke harshly to them. "Where do you come from?" he said. They said, "From the land of Canaan, to buy food." ⁸Although Joseph had recognized his brothers, they did not recognize him. ⁹Joseph also remembered the dreams that he had dreamed about them. He said to them, "You are spies; you have come to see the nakedness of the land!" ¹⁰They said to him, "No, my lord; your servants have come to buy food. ¹¹We are all sons of one man; we are honest men; your servants have never been spies." ¹²But he said to them, "No, you have come to see the nakedness of the land!" ¹³They said, "We, your servants, are twelve

brothers, the sons of a certain man in the land of Canaan; the youngest, however, is now with our father, and one is no more." ¹⁴But Joseph said to them, "It is just as I have said to you; you are spies! ¹⁵Here is how you shall be tested: as Pharaoh lives, you shall not leave this place unless your youngest brother comes here! ¹⁶Let one of you go and bring your brother, while the rest of you remain in prison, in order that your words may be tested, whether there is truth in you; or else, as Pharaoh lives, surely you are spies." ¹⁷And he put them all together in prison for three days. ¹⁸On the third day Joseph said to them, "Do this and you will live, for I fear God: ¹⁹if you are honest men, let one of your brothers stay here where you are imprisoned. The rest of you shall go and carry grain for the famine of your households, ²⁰and bring your youngest brother to me. Thus your words will be verified, and you shall not die." And they agreed to do so.

²¹They said to one another, "Alas, we are paying the penalty for what we did to our brother; we saw his anguish when he pleaded with us, but we would not listen. That is why this anguish has come upon us." ²²Then Reuben answered them, "Did I not tell you not to wrong the boy? But you would not listen. So now there comes a reckoning for his blood." ²³They did not know that Joseph understood them, since he spoke with them through an interpreter. ²⁴He turned away from them and wept; then he returned and spoke to them. And he picked out Simeon and had him bound before their eyes. ²⁵Joseph then gave orders to fill their bags with grain, to return every man's money to his sack, and to give them provisions for their journey. This was done for them. ²⁶They loaded their donkeys with their grain, and departed. ²⁷When

A Journey through Genesis

one of them opened his sack to give his donkey fodder at the lodging place, he saw his money at the top of the sack. ²⁸He said to his brothers, "My money has been put back; here it is in my sack!" At this they lost heart and turned trembling to one another, saying, "What is this that God has done to us?"

²⁹When they came to their father Jacob in the land of Canaan, they told him all that had happened to them, saying, ³⁰"The man, the lord of the land, spoke harshly to us, and charged us with spying on the land. ³¹But we said to him, 'We are honest men, we are not spies. ³²We are twelve brothers, sons of our father; one is no more, and the youngest is now with our father in the land of Canaan.' ³³Then the man, the lord of the land, said to us, 'By this I shall know that you are honest men: leave one of your brothers with me, take grain for the famine of your households, and go your way. ³⁴Bring your youngest

brother to me, and I shall know that you are not spies but honest men. Then I will release your brother to you, and you may trade in the land.'" ³⁵As they were emptying their sacks, there in each one's sack was his bag of money. When they and their father saw their bundles of money, they were dismayed. ³⁶And their father Jacob said to them, "I am the one you have bereaved of children: Joseph is no more, and Simeon is no more, and now you would take Benjamin. All this has happened to me!" ³⁷Then Reuben said to his father, "You may kill my two sons if I do not bring him back to you. Put him in my hands, and I will bring him back to you." ³⁸But he said, "My son shall not go down with you, for his brother is dead, and he alone is left. If harm should come to him on the journey that you are to make, you would bring down my gray hairs with sorrow to Sheol."

Reflection

In 1963, Civil Rights leader Fannie Lou Hamer was arrested and placed in jail. While imprisoned, white guards forced two fellow prisoners to beat her to the brink of death. When she was regaining consciousness, Hamer heard the guards state that they could throw her in the river, and no one would ever find her.

You must have to rob someone of their humanity before you can treat them like that. You must refuse to see the face of God in someone to consider them, and their lives, disposable. You can't suggest the disposal of someone if you believe that they are a child of God, just like you, a sibling in Christ.

Joseph's brothers left him to die in a ditch, only pulling him out to sell him for 20 pieces of silver. They had to have reached a point in which they no longer saw their brother but simply an "other" needing to be disposed.

When the brothers come to Joseph asking for food to save them from starvation, they don't recognize him. All they see is someone who has something they desperately need. Joseph's testing of his brothers reminds them of their past brokenness, and they begin to fight among each other as to who is to blame for their current affliction. They fracture under the weight of their guilt.

I wonder if Joseph's test, following the tears he shed as he listened to them, was designed to see not if they were spies but if they could somehow remember what it means to see the beloved humanity in each other. I wonder if this was a test to see if they were capable of feeling the brokenness that comes when we separate ourselves from those with whom God binds us.

Reconciliation, healing, and wholeness is what God wants for each one of us. God stirs our hearts and asks us to see one another as the beloved children of God that we are. In God's economy, no one is disposable. In God's heart, there is no "other," only "all in all."

— **The Rt. Rev. Jeffrey W. Mello**

Questions

For what, or with whom, do you seek reconciliation? What might God be inviting you to do so that you might know the healing and wholeness that God longs to give?

Every day we see examples in our lives and in the world of people who have separated themselves, or attempted to separate others, from the divine siblinghood. Who is "other" to you? How might God be calling you to see them in a new way, as beloved children of God, just like you?

In our baptismal covenant, we promise to "respect the dignity of every human being." How might you practice that throughout your day? What might that look like for you?

Prayer

Loving God, you have made us in your image, and you have made us one people in your name. Help us to see your face in the face of each person we meet, that we might live together in the fullness of your grace and love. Give us the will to love one another as you intend and as your Son commanded. *Amen.*

Genesis 43

43 Now the famine was severe in the land. ²And when they had eaten up the grain that they had brought from Egypt, their father said to them, "Go again, buy us a little more food." ³But Judah said to him, "The man solemnly warned us, saying, 'You shall not see my face unless your brother is with you.' ⁴If you will send our brother with us, we will go down and buy you food; ⁵but if you will not send him, we will not go down, for the man said to us, 'You shall not see my face, unless your brother is with you.'" ⁶Israel said, "Why did you treat me so badly as to tell the man that you had another brother?" ⁷They replied, "The man questioned us carefully about ourselves and our kindred, saying, 'Is your father still alive? Have you another brother?' What we told him was in answer to these questions. Could we in any way know that he would say, 'Bring your brother down'?" ⁸Then Judah said to his father Israel, "Send the boy with me, and let us be on our way, so that we may live and not die—you and we and also our little ones. ⁹I myself will be surety for him; you can hold me accountable for him. If I do not bring him back to you and set him before you, then let me bear the blame forever. ¹⁰If we had not delayed, we would now have returned twice."

¹¹Then their father Israel said to them, "If it must be so, then do this: take some of the choice fruits of the land in your bags, and carry them down as a present to the man—a little balm and a little honey, gum, resin,

pistachio nuts, and almonds. [12]Take double the money with you. Carry back with you the money that was returned in the top of your sacks; perhaps it was an oversight. [13]Take your brother also, and be on your way again to the man; [14]may God Almighty grant you mercy before the man, so that he may send back your other brother and Benjamin. As for me, if I am bereaved of my children, I am bereaved."

[15]So the men took the present, and they took double the money with them, as well as Benjamin. Then they went on their way down to Egypt, and stood before Joseph. [16]When Joseph saw Benjamin with them, he said to the steward of his house, "Bring the men into the house, and slaughter an animal and make ready, for the men are to dine with me at noon." [17]The man did as Joseph said, and brought the men to Joseph's house. [18]Now the men were afraid because they were brought to Joseph's house, and they said, "It is because of the money, replaced in our sacks the first time, that we have been brought in, so that he may have an opportunity to fall upon us, to make slaves of us and take our donkeys." [19]So they went up to the steward of Joseph's house and spoke with him at the entrance to the house. [20]They said, "Oh, my lord, we came down the first time to buy food; [21]and when we came to the lodging place we opened our sacks, and there was each one's money in the top of his sack, our money in full weight. So we have brought it back with us. [22]Moreover we have brought down with us additional money to buy food. We do not know who put our money in our sacks." [23]He replied, "Rest assured, do not be afraid; your God and the God of your father must have put treasure in your sacks for you; I received

your money." Then he brought Simeon out to them. ²⁴When the steward had brought the men into Joseph's house, and given them water, and they had washed their feet, and when he had given their donkeys fodder, ²⁵they made the present ready for Joseph's coming at noon, for they had heard that they would dine there.

²⁶When Joseph came home, they brought him the present that they had carried into the house, and bowed to the ground before him. ²⁷He inquired about their welfare, and said, "Is your father well, the old man of whom you spoke? Is he still alive?" ²⁸They said, "Your servant our father is well; he is still alive." And they bowed their heads and did obeisance. ²⁹Then he looked up and saw his brother Benjamin, his mother's son, and said, "Is this your youngest brother, of whom you spoke to me? God be gracious to you, my son!"

³⁰With that, Joseph hurried out, because he was overcome with affection for his brother, and he was about to weep. So he went into a private room and wept there. ³¹Then he washed his face and came out; and controlling himself he said, "Serve the meal." ³²They served him by himself, and them by themselves, and the Egyptians who ate with him by themselves, because the Egyptians could not eat with the Hebrews, for that is an abomination to the Egyptians. ³³When they were seated before him, the firstborn according to his birthright and the youngest according to his youth, the men looked at one another in amazement. ³⁴Portions were taken to them from Joseph's table, but Benjamin's portion was five times as much as any of theirs. So they drank and were merry with him.

Reflection

Healing takes time. Reconciliation is often hard work.

Not unlike the healing miracle in Mark 8, where Jesus heals a blind man in two stages, so too we see the relationship between Joseph and his brothers healing bit by bit. Like many things in life, healing turns out to be a process.

The chapter opens with Judah and his brothers returning to Egypt, this time with Benjamin in tow. Israel (Jacob) had not wanted to let him go for fear of losing the only other son born of his beloved wife, Rachel. Judah persuades him, but Israel rightly recognizes the perils involved and so prays that God's mercy will go with them. Israel is bereaved, but he also recognizes he has no choice.

Upon arriving in Egypt, the brothers are met not by Joseph but by his steward, who is the first to extend shalom, a welcome and word of peace. They have proven trustworthy by returning as they had promised, not just with Benjamin but also with double the money they had found in their sacks on the way out of Egypt.

The steward's shalom is echoed by Joseph's own when he comes out to meet his brothers, although all is not yet forgiven. Trust so powerfully broken cannot be restored that easily. Joseph maintains a level of distance and guardedness that is understandable, if not what he or we might hope for him. He excuses himself when overcome with emotion at the sight of Benjamin, lest he become vulnerable and reveal his true feelings. The brothers bow down before him, a posture of obeisance typically reserved for God alone.

And when the feast is laid, it is no happy family meal. Egyptians and Hebrews are served separately, and Joseph still does not reveal his identity to them.

Throughout, Joseph's messy and complicated humanity is on full display. And yet his desire for reconciliation, healing, and peace is no less real. He presses on. Even if he requires one more test.

— The Rev. Ryan Fleenor

Questions

Where do you struggle to practice compassion, reconciliation, and forgiveness?

Where do you struggle to receive compassion, reconciliation, and forgiveness?

What helps you rebuild trust after it's broken?

Prayer

God of peace, you come to gather us into one reconciled and healed human family: Give us your Spirit and a measure of your grace, that we may accomplish your will and experience your peace amidst the things that divide and confound us. Make us instruments of your peace. *Amen.*

Genesis 44

44 Then he commanded the steward of his house, "Fill the men's sacks with food, as much as they can carry, and put each man's money in the top of his sack. [2]Put my cup, the silver cup, in the top of the sack of the youngest, with his money for the grain." And he did as Joseph told him. [3]As soon as the morning was light, the men were sent away with their donkeys. [4]When they had gone only a short distance from the city, Joseph said to his steward, "Go, follow after the men; and when you overtake them, say to them, 'Why have you returned evil for good? Why have you stolen my silver cup? [5]Is it not from this that my lord drinks? Does he not indeed use it for divination? You have done wrong in doing this.'" [6]When he overtook them, he repeated these words to them. [7]They said to him, "Why does my lord speak such words as these? Far be it from your servants that they should do such a thing! [8]Look, the money that we found at the top of our sacks, we brought back to you from the land of Canaan; why then would we steal silver or gold from your lord's house? [9]Should it be found with any one of your servants, let him die; moreover the rest of us will become my lord's slaves." [10]He said, "Even so; in accordance with your words, let it be: he with whom it is found shall become my slave, but the rest of you shall go free." [11]Then each one quickly lowered his sack to the ground, and each opened his sack. [12]He searched, beginning with the eldest and ending with the youngest; and the cup was found in Benjamin's sack. [13]At this they tore their clothes. Then each one loaded

his donkey, and they returned to the city. ¹⁴Judah and his brothers came to Joseph's house while he was still there; and they fell to the ground before him. ¹⁵Joseph said to them, "What deed is this that you have done? Do you not know that one such as I can practice divination?" ¹⁶And Judah said, "What can we say to my lord? What can we speak? How can we clear ourselves? God has found out the guilt of your servants; here we are then, my lord's slaves, both we and also the one in whose possession the cup has been found." ¹⁷But he said, "Far be it from me that I should do so! Only the one in whose possession the cup was found shall be my slave; but as for you, go up in peace to your father."

¹⁸Then Judah stepped up to him and said, "O my lord, let your servant please speak a word in my lord's ears, and do not be angry with your servant; for you are like Pharaoh himself. ¹⁹My lord asked his servants, saying, 'Have you a father or a brother?' ²⁰And we said to my lord, 'We have a father, an old man, and a young brother, the child of his old age. His brother is dead; he alone is left of his mother's children, and his father loves him.' ²¹Then you said to your servants, 'Bring him down to me, so that I may set my eyes on him.' ²²We said to my lord, 'The boy cannot leave his father, for if he should leave his father, his father would die.' ²³Then you said to your servants, 'Unless your youngest brother comes down with you, you shall see my face no more.' ²⁴When we went back to your servant my father we told him the words of my lord. ²⁵And when our father said, 'Go again, buy us a little food,' ²⁶we said, 'We cannot go down. Only if our youngest brother goes with us, will we go down; for we cannot see the man's face unless our youngest brother is with us.' ²⁷Then your

servant my father said to us, 'You know that my wife bore me two sons; ²⁸one left me, and I said, Surely he has been torn to pieces; and I have never seen him since. ²⁹If you take this one also from me, and harm comes to him, you will bring down my gray hairs in sorrow to Sheol.' ³⁰Now therefore, when I come to your servant my father and the boy is not with us, then, as his life is bound up in the boy's life, ³¹when he sees that the boy is not with us, he will die; and your servants will bring down the gray hairs of your servant our father with sorrow to Sheol. ³²For your servant became surety for the boy to my father, saying, 'If I do not bring him back to you, then I will bear the blame in the sight of my father all my life.' ³³Now therefore, please let your servant remain as a slave to my lord in place of the boy; and let the boy go back with his brothers. ³⁴For how can I go back to my father if the boy is not with me? I fear to see the suffering that would come upon my father."

Reflection

One final test indeed. The entire saga of Joseph and his brothers, which began back in chapter 37, is finally reaching its climax.

Joseph sends his brothers on their way back to Canaan with ample food and money, but in Benjamin's sack he plants one additional item: a silver cup that, when discovered, will reveal his brothers' true colors.

As planned, the brothers are not long on the road when Joseph's steward catches up with them and "discovers" the silver cup. Back to Joseph they all go, and quickly Judah emerges as the brothers' chief spokesperson. His response to Joseph's accusations is the longest—and perhaps most moving—speech in all of Genesis.

Unlike in chapter 37, when his response to the plot to kill Joseph is to have him sold into slavery, Judah here shows greater moral courage. Joseph wants to keep Benjamin with him in Egypt, but Judah offers himself instead, a sacrifice that would benefit both Benjamin and his heartbroken father, Israel, who cannot bear to lose another of Rachel's sons.

Watching Judah take that risk on behalf of his father and brother no doubt plays a role in Joseph deciding to take his own risk and reveal his true identity in the next chapter. But I think he is equally moved to hear Judah openly confess the truth of his wrongdoing. The brothers have previously acknowledged their guilt to one another (Genesis 42:21); now they speak the truth in Joseph's presence (44:16).

Our human family is no less divided and conflicted than Joseph and his brothers. As followers of Jesus, who came that we might share in his ministry of reconciliation, what can we learn from this story? How might Judah's example inspire us? I think it comes down to those two actions: being willing to tell the truth (and confess our fault when necessary) and being willing to step back from our privilege and put the well-being of others front and center. Like Judah, these actions just might help move us closer to one another and to God.

— The Rev. Ryan Fleenor

Questions

Has there been a time when speaking the truth, even a difficult truth, has set you free?

In what ways might you be called to decrease so that others might increase?

Prayer

Reconciling and forgiving God, give us grace to follow always in the footsteps of Christ, who came not to be served, but to serve. Keep us faithful to his ministry of reconciliation, and kindle in our hearts the fire of his love for each and for all. *Amen.*

Genesis 45

45 Then Joseph could no longer control himself before all those who stood by him, and he cried out, "Send everyone away from me." So no one stayed with him when Joseph made himself known to his brothers. ²And he wept so loudly that the Egyptians heard it, and the household of Pharaoh heard it. ³Joseph said to his brothers, "I am Joseph. Is my father still alive?" But his brothers could not answer him, so dismayed were they at his presence. ⁴Then Joseph said to his brothers, "Come closer to me." And they came closer. He said, "I am your brother, Joseph, whom you sold into Egypt. ⁵And now do not be distressed, or angry with yourselves, because you sold me here; for God sent me before you to preserve life. ⁶For the famine has been in the land these two years; and there are five more years in which there will be neither plowing nor harvest. ⁷God sent me before you to preserve for you a remnant on earth, and to keep alive for you many survivors. ⁸So it was not you who sent me here, but God; he has made me a father to Pharaoh, and lord of all his house and ruler over all the land of Egypt. ⁹Hurry and go up to my father and say to him, 'Thus says your son Joseph, God has made me lord of all Egypt; come down to me, do not delay. ¹⁰You shall settle in the land of Goshen, and you shall be near me, you and your children and your children's children, as well as your flocks, your herds, and all that you have. ¹¹I will provide for you there—since there are five more years of famine to come—so that you and your

household, and all that you have, will not come to poverty.' [12]And now your eyes and the eyes of my brother Benjamin see that it is my own mouth that speaks to you. [13]You must tell my father how greatly I am honored in Egypt, and all that you have seen. Hurry and bring my father down here." [14]Then he fell upon his brother Benjamin's neck and wept, while Benjamin wept upon his neck. [15]And he kissed all his brothers and wept upon them; and after that his brothers talked with him.

[16]When the report was heard in Pharaoh's house, "Joseph's brothers have come," Pharaoh and his servants were pleased. [17]Pharaoh said to Joseph, "Say to your brothers, 'Do this: load your animals and go back to the land of Canaan. [18]Take your father and your households and come to me, so that I may give you the best of the land of Egypt, and you may enjoy the fat of the land.' [19]You are further charged to say, 'Do this: take wagons from the land of Egypt for your little ones and for your wives, and bring your father, and come. [20]Give no thought to your possessions, for the best of all the land of Egypt is yours.'" [21]The sons of Israel did so. Joseph gave them wagons according to the instruction of Pharaoh, and he gave them provisions for the journey. [22]To each one of them he gave a set of garments; but to Benjamin he gave three hundred pieces of silver and five sets of garments. [23]To his father he sent the following: ten donkeys loaded with the good things of Egypt, and ten female donkeys loaded with grain, bread, and provision for his father on the journey. [24]Then he sent his brothers on their way, and as they were leaving he said to them, "Do not quarrel along the way."

[25]So they went up out of Egypt and came to their father Jacob in the land of Canaan. [26]And

they told him, "Joseph is still alive! He is even ruler over all the land of Egypt." He was stunned; he could not believe them. ²⁷But when they told him all the words of Joseph that he had said to them, and when he saw the wagons that Joseph had sent to carry him, the spirit of their father Jacob revived. ²⁸Israel said, "Enough! My son Joseph is still alive. I must go and see him before I die."

Reflection

It usually seems easier to worship God and to give God thanks when things go well. But how do we give thanks and praise when terrible things happen?

And when someone does something cruel and damaging to us, how are we supposed to forgive them, especially if they have not asked for forgiveness?

In this chapter, we see a different way, one which can be life-giving. After some time, Joseph finally reveals himself to his brothers. He sends everyone else away and tells them who he is. They are dismayed and distressed, certain that he will now punish them for selling him into slavery, which would be a reasonable response! They feel guilty and frightened. But Joseph's reaction is extraordinary. He asks, "Is my father still alive?", immediately re-establishing their familial relationship. And he hurries on to tell them, "Do not be distressed, or angry with yourselves, because you sold me here; for God sent me before you to preserve life…it was not you who sent me here, but God" (Genesis 45:5-8).

Joseph sees God's hand in the terrible events that sent him to Egypt. He sees himself as God's instrument to preserve life, "to keep alive for you many survivors." Moreover, he has not allowed himself to nourish bitterness over the years; he "kissed all his brothers and wept upon them." Because Joseph sees God at work constantly, he is able to forgive and reconcile with his brothers, re-establish relationship, and bring his extended family to Egypt in the time of famine.

What Joseph's brothers did was wrong. But Joseph had a choice, as we have a choice. He chose to believe that there was no place or circumstances where God was not, and in his years in Egypt, he found God in slavery, in prison, and in a time, a famine. He did not nourish and build his resentment; he remained open to God's purposes and became part of them.

— **The Very Rev. Lucinda Laird**

Questions _____

Do you think God causes bad things to happen? Or does God use all situations, no matter how bad, to be open to grace?

How can you remain open to God's presence when you are hurting or frightened? Can you keep praying even if it feels like no one is listening?

Can you work on not allowing resentment or anger to close your eyes to forgiveness and new hope?

Prayer _____

Gracious God, in Jesus, you showed us what love in human form looks like. Help us to grow into his image that we may learn to love more and more and to forgive freely. When we are hurt, angry or frightened, open our eyes to see you and to believe that you can use all the circumstances of our lives for good. *Amen.*

Genesis 46

46 When Israel set out on his journey with all that he had and came to Beer-sheba, he offered sacrifices to the God of his father Isaac. ²God spoke to Israel in visions of the night, and said, "Jacob, Jacob." And he said, "Here I am." ³Then he said, "I am God, the God of your father; do not be afraid to go down to Egypt, for I will make of you a great nation there. ⁴I myself will go down with you to Egypt, and I will also bring you up again; and Joseph's own hand shall close your eyes."

⁵Then Jacob set out from Beer-sheba; and the sons of Israel carried their father Jacob, their little ones, and their wives, in the wagons that Pharaoh had sent to carry him. ⁶They also took their livestock and the goods that they had acquired in the land of Canaan, and they came into Egypt, Jacob and all his offspring with him, ⁷his sons, and his sons' sons with him, his daughters, and his sons' daughters; all his offspring he brought with him into Egypt. ⁸Now these are the names of the Israelites, Jacob and his offspring, who came to Egypt. Reuben, Jacob's firstborn, ⁹and the children of Reuben: Hanoch, Pallu, Hezron, and Carmi. ¹⁰The children of Simeon: Jemuel, Jamin, Ohad, Jachin, Zohar, and Shaul, the son of a Canaanite woman. ¹¹The children of Levi: Gershon, Kohath, and Merari. ¹²The children of Judah: Er, Onan, Shelah, Perez, and Zerah (but Er and Onan died in the land of Canaan); and the children of Perez were Hezron and Hamul. ¹³The children of Issachar: Tola,

Puvah, Jashub, and Shimron. [14]The children of Zebulun: Sered, Elon, and Jahleel [15](these are the sons of Leah, whom she bore to Jacob in Paddan-aram, together with his daughter Dinah; in all his sons and his daughters numbered thirty-three). [16]The children of Gad: Ziphion, Haggi, Shuni, Ezbon, Eri, Arodi, and Areli. [17]The children of Asher: Imnah, Ishvah, Ishvi, Beriah, and their sister Serah. The children of Beriah: Heber and Malchiel [18](these are the children of Zilpah, whom Laban gave to his daughter Leah; and these she bore to Jacob—sixteen persons). [19]The children of Jacob's wife Rachel: Joseph and Benjamin. [20]To Joseph in the land of Egypt were born Manasseh and Ephraim, whom Asenath daughter of Potiphera, priest of On, bore to him. [21]The children of Benjamin: Bela, Becher, Ashbel, Gera, Naaman, Ehi, Rosh, Muppim, Huppim, and Ard [22](these are the children of Rachel, who were born to Jacob—fourteen persons in all). [23]The children of Dan: Hashum. [24]The children of Naphtali: Jahzeel, Guni, Jezer, and Shillem [25](these are the children of Bilhah, whom Laban gave to his daughter Rachel, and these she bore to Jacob—seven persons in all). [26]All the persons belonging to Jacob who came into Egypt, who were his own offspring, not including the wives of his sons, were sixty-six persons in all. [27]The children of Joseph, who were born to him in Egypt, were two; all the persons of the house of Jacob who came into Egypt were seventy.

[28]Israel sent Judah ahead to Joseph to lead the way before him into Goshen. When they came to the land of Goshen, [29]Joseph made ready his chariot and went up to meet his father Israel in Goshen. He presented himself to him, fell on his neck, and wept on his neck a good

while. [30]Israel said to Joseph, "I can die now, having seen for myself that you are still alive." [31]Joseph said to his brothers and to his father's household, "I will go up and tell Pharaoh, and will say to him, 'My brothers and my father's household, who were in the land of Canaan, have come to me. [32]The men are shepherds, for they have been keepers of livestock; and they have brought their flocks, and their herds, and all that they have.' [33]When Pharaoh calls you, and says, 'What is your occupation?' [34]you shall say, 'Your servants have been keepers of livestock from our youth even until now, both we and our ancestors' — in order that you may settle in the land of Goshen, because all shepherds are abhorrent to the Egyptians."

Reflection

Ten years ago, I received a call to be the dean of the American Cathedral in Paris, and I moved from Louisville, Kentucky, to France. About two weeks before I left, I had a huge anxiety attack. I realized I had quit my job, sold my house, shipped my belongings to Paris, and was about to go to a country where I knew no one and spoke the language very poorly. What was I thinking? (Suffice it to say that it all turned out well, but I remember being very, very scared.)

In this chapter, Israel (Jacob) sets "out on his journey with all that he had." He offers sacrifice to God, and God speaks to him, telling him not to be afraid, promising to be with him, and assuring him that this is the right thing to do. He goes to Egypt with all of his livestock, possessions, and children and grandchildren. The rest of the chapter is very practical: lots and lots of names of all the people who traveled with him and a description of Joseph's meeting them in Goshen and making arrangements for their arrival in Egypt.

God reassures Jacob before he asks, probably knowing full well how frightening this huge change would be for him and the 66 other people traveling with him. They were setting off into the unknown. But they were doing so in faith, as Abraham had done, and in hope of something more. As Hebrews 11:16 says, "they desire a better country, that is, a heavenly one. Therefore God…has prepared a city for them."

Perhaps we've all experienced a time when we have set off into the unknown by faith and left the familiar behind. How do we know if

A Journey through Genesis

it is the right thing to do? How do we know if God is really calling us? Sometimes, to be sure, we make mistakes, we fail. Being anxious or scared is part of being human. But faith is not certainty; it is a relationship of trust. We trust that God will be with us, no matter where our journey leads.

— **The Very Rev. Lucinda Laird**

Questions

Can you remember a time when you set off into the unknown or changed your life dramatically? Were you ever 100% sure about it?

God does speak to us but sometimes in ways we aren't too sure about. Can you keep praying that you will recognize God's call?

Perhaps one path is as good as another at various times in our lives, but what's important is that we walk with God. Can you pray for open ears, eyes, and heart to be aware of God at work in everything you do?

Prayer

Holy God, we ask for wisdom and discernment to know what you would have us do and the courage to do it. Lead us in hope and trust. Bring us closer and closer to you in the journey of our lives, the journey to and with and into you. *Amen.*

Genesis 47

47 So Joseph went and told Pharaoh, "My father and my brothers, with their flocks and herds and all that they possess, have come from the land of Canaan; they are now in the land of Goshen." [2]From among his brothers he took five men and presented them to Pharaoh. [3]Pharaoh said to his brothers, "What is your occupation?" And they said to Pharaoh, "Your servants are shepherds, as our ancestors were." [4]They said to Pharaoh, "We have come to reside as aliens in the land; for there is no pasture for your servants' flocks because the famine is severe in the land of Canaan. Now, we ask you, let your servants settle in the land of Goshen." [5]Then Pharaoh said to Joseph, "Your father and your brothers have come to you. [6]The land of Egypt is before you; settle your father and your brothers in the best part of the land; let them live in the land of Goshen; and if you know that there are capable men among them, put them in charge of my livestock." [7]Then Joseph brought in his father Jacob, and presented him before Pharaoh, and Jacob blessed Pharaoh. [8]Pharaoh said to Jacob, "How many are the years of your life?" [9]Jacob said to Pharaoh, "The years of my earthly sojourn are one hundred thirty; few and hard have been the years of my life. They do not compare with the years of the life of my ancestors during their long sojourn." [10]Then Jacob blessed Pharaoh, and went out from the presence of Pharaoh. [11]Joseph settled his father and his brothers, and granted them a holding in the land of Egypt, in the best part of the land, in the land of Rameses, as Pharaoh

had instructed. ¹²And Joseph provided his father, his brothers, and all his father's household with food, according to the number of their dependents.

¹³Now there was no food in all the land, for the famine was very severe. The land of Egypt and the land of Canaan languished because of the famine. ¹⁴Joseph collected all the money to be found in the land of Egypt and in the land of Canaan, in exchange for the grain that they bought; and Joseph brought the money into Pharaoh's house. ¹⁵When the money from the land of Egypt and from the land of Canaan was spent, all the Egyptians came to Joseph, and said, "Give us food! Why should we die before your eyes? For our money is gone." ¹⁶And Joseph answered, "Give me your livestock, and I will give you food in exchange for your livestock, if your money is gone." ¹⁷So they brought their livestock to Joseph; and Joseph gave them food in exchange for the horses, the flocks, the herds, and the donkeys. That year he supplied them with food in exchange for all their livestock. ¹⁸When that year was ended, they came to him the following year, and said to him, "We can not hide from my lord that our money is all spent; and the herds of cattle are my lord's. There is nothing left in the sight of my lord but our bodies and our lands. ¹⁹Shall we die before your eyes, both we and our land? Buy us and our land in exchange for food. We with our land will become slaves to Pharaoh; just give us seed, so that we may live and not die, and that the land may not become desolate." ²⁰So Joseph bought all the land of Egypt for Pharaoh. All the Egyptians sold their fields, because the famine was severe upon them; and the land became Pharaoh's. ²¹As for the people, he made slaves of them from one end of Egypt to the other. ²²Only the land of the priests he did not buy; for

the priests had a fixed allowance from Pharaoh, and lived on the allowance that Pharaoh gave them; therefore they did not sell their land. ²³Then Joseph said to the people, "Now that I have this day bought you and your land for Pharaoh, here is seed for you; sow the land. ²⁴And at the harvests you shall give one-fifth to Pharaoh, and four-fifths shall be your own, as seed for the field and as food for yourselves and your households, and as food for your little ones." ²⁵They said, "You have saved our lives; may it please my lord, we will be slaves to Pharaoh." ²⁶So Joseph made it a statute concerning the land of Egypt, and it stands to this day, that Pharaoh should have the fifth. The land of the priests alone did not become Pharaoh's.

²⁷Thus Israel settled in the land of Egypt, in the region of Goshen; and they gained possessions in it, and were fruitful and multiplied exceedingly. ²⁸Jacob lived in the land of Egypt seventeen years; so the days of Jacob, the years of his life, were one hundred forty-seven years. ²⁹When the time of Israel's death drew near, he called his son Joseph and said to him, "If I have found favor with you, put your hand under my thigh and promise to deal loyally and truly with me. Do not bury me in Egypt. ³⁰When I lie down with my ancestors, carry me out of Egypt and bury me in their burial place." He answered, "I will do as you have said." ³¹And he said, "Swear to me"; and he swore to him. Then Israel bowed himself on the head of his bed.

Reflection

When we were children, many of us measured our ages, not just in years but in half-years or three-quarter years as in "I'm five and a half years old." It was a way to compare ourselves to others and provide some measure of what we had achieved in life. My beloved 97-year-old mother-in-law has recently returned to telling how old she is in every conversation by stating that "I'm in my ninety-eighth year." We're pretty sure it's both a matter of pride and a reminder to give her a break when she forgets something she's known all her life. Age is relative, of course, and it rarely helps to define who we are or what we know or what our interests might be and certainly age has nothing to do with the quality of our hearts and the life we have known. In fact, age may be one the shallowest measures one can conjure.

In this chapter of Genesis, we see Jacob restored to all of his sons, including Joseph who he believed dead for years. The family is restored and has been given a place in Pharaoh's kingdom to ride out the famine and to take responsibility for Pharaoh's own flocks. Joseph brings the family of the promise of God to present them to Pharoah, petitioners brought before the power of all Egypt, and Pharoah asks Jacob a question: "How old are you?" With all the questions he might ask of the father of Joseph who has saved Egypt from the famine, Pharoah asks about Jacob's age.

Jacob gives his age, but he describes it not merely in years but by a quality of his life. The head of the family of the promise of God replies that his sojourn has been 130 years. Jacob is speaking to something more powerful and important than mere counting. He is speaking of his life's journey with God and to this God who has watched over him and guided him and loved him, even when he was not all that lovable. Then the text states that Jacob blesses Pharoah. It's hard to know whether it is the older blessing the younger or whether it is the one touched by the promise of God sharing that promise with another. I like to think it is the latter.

We can't really measure our sojourns in years alone, nor does God grant many of us a steady progression of spiritual insight and experience day by day. Instead, our lives with God are marked more by moments, insights, revelations, and dry spots that shape us in ways that have very little to do with the passage of time and more to do with the grace and the promise and the presence of God.

— **The Rev. W. Frank Allen**

Questions

What are the most important ages in your life? What about those ages speaks to the person you are and the person you are becoming?

Instead of measuring by years, how can we look at our lives as journeying with and to God?

Prayer

Gracious God, we thank you for this day, for its triumphs and challenges. Teach us to measure our days by your presence and grace and not merely by time, that we may be drawn closer to your heart and your call on our lives. All this we ask through the name of Jesus Christ our Lord, who lives and reigns with you and the Holy Spirit, one God, now and forever. *Amen.*

Day 48

Genesis 48

48 After this Joseph was told, "Your father is ill." So he took with him his two sons, Manasseh and Ephraim. ²When Jacob was told, "Your son Joseph has come to you," he summoned his strength and sat up in bed. ³And Jacob said to Joseph, "God Almighty appeared to me at Luz in the land of Canaan, and he blessed me, ⁴and said to me, 'I am going to make you fruitful and increase your numbers; I will make of you a company of peoples, and will give this land to your offspring after you for a perpetual holding.' ⁵Therefore your two sons, who were born to you in the land of Egypt before I came to you in Egypt, are now mine; Ephraim and Manasseh shall be mine, just as Reuben and Simeon are. ⁶As for the offspring born to you after them, they shall be yours.

They shall be recorded under the names of their brothers with regard to their inheritance. ⁷For when I came from Paddan, Rachel, alas, died in the land of Canaan on the way, while there was still some distance to go to Ephrath; and I buried her there on the way to Ephrath" (that is, Bethlehem).

⁸When Israel saw Joseph's sons, he said, "Who are these?" ⁹Joseph said to his father, "They are my sons, whom God has given me here." And he said, "Bring them to me, please, that I may bless them." ¹⁰Now the eyes of Israel were dim with age, and he could not see well. So Joseph brought them near him; and he kissed them and embraced them. ¹¹Israel said to Joseph, "I did not expect to see your face; and here God has let me see your children

also." [12]Then Joseph removed them from his father's knees, and he bowed himself with his face to the earth. [13]Joseph took them both, Ephraim in his right hand toward Israel's left, and Manasseh in his left hand toward Israel's right, and brought them near him. [14]But Israel stretched out his right hand and laid it on the head of Ephraim, who was the younger, and his left hand on the head of Manasseh, crossing his hands, for Manasseh was the firstborn. [15]He blessed Joseph, and said, "The God before whom my ancestors Abraham and Isaac walked, the God who has been my shepherd all my life to this day, [16]the angel who has redeemed me from all harm, bless the boys; and in them let my name be perpetuated, and the name of my ancestors Abraham and Isaac; and let them grow into a multitude on the earth." [17]When Joseph saw that his father laid his right hand on the head of Ephraim,

it displeased him; so he took his father's hand, to remove it from Ephraim's head to Manasseh's head. [18]Joseph said to his father, "Not so, my father! Since this one is the firstborn, put your right hand on his head." [19]But his father refused, and said, "I know, my son, I know; he also shall become a people, and he also shall be great. Nevertheless his younger brother shall be greater than he, and his offspring shall become a multitude of nations." [20]So he blessed them that day, saying, "By you Israel will invoke blessings, saying, 'God make you like Ephraim and like Manasseh.'" So he put Ephraim ahead of Manasseh. [21]Then Israel said to Joseph, "I am about to die, but God will be with you and will bring you again to the land of your ancestors. [22]I now give to you one portion more than to your brothers, the portion that I took from the hand of the Amorites with my sword and with my bow."

Reflection

Christians and those seeking God ask in the Lord's Prayer for God's will to be done on earth as it is in heaven. This part of the Lord's Prayer is both a surrender to God's gracious hand and vision for our lives and the world and a reminder that what God has in mind and what God is seeking in our lives and the life of the world is not always what we may be seeking. God often has a different end in mind. And though we must be careful about claiming we know God's will, living into God's will, even though it is often different than we expect, is the path to true life.

In this passage, Jacob has reached the end of his life, and Joseph determines to bring his sons, Ephraim and Manasseh, to be blessed by the head of the family of the promise of God. Jacob recounts his sojourn with God to Joseph and his sons and the promise God makes to Jacob and his family. Jacob then turns to Joseph's sons to give them each the blessing of God. Jacob reaches out his hands and places his right hand on the younger son, Ephraim, to receive the first blessing and his left hand on the older son, Manasseh. In the midst of the blessing, Joseph attempts to correct his father in blessing the younger over the elder, in keeping with the practice of first sons holding the greater position. Jacob, with some apparent foreknowledge of God's will, reverses the tradition and explains to Joseph that in God's vision, the younger will be greater than the elder. Both sons are blessed.

God's will is often different than our wills or our expectations. And the reversal in first blessing we see in this story is a theme throughout the Bible, especially when we meet Jesus. Jesus is constantly reversing the norms of the day, calling us to pray for and love our enemies, revealing God's blessings in times of distress, calling us to be servants of all as the measure of true greatness, and breaking the hold and power of death on Easter as the sign of God's ultimate will for humanity and all of God's creation.

— The Rev. W. Frank Allen

Questions

When have you experienced God's will in your life? In the lives of those you love? In the life of the world?

When have you experienced God's reversal or unexpected will and vision in your life?

Prayer

Loving God, we thank you that you are involved in our lives in personal and in general ways. Open our hearts and lives to your will and give us a deep sense of confidence and hope that you are guiding us along the right paths, even though we may know nothing about it. Grant this and all our prayers for your good purposes and in the praise of your Holy Name. *Amen.*

Genesis 49

49 Then Jacob called his sons, and said: "Gather around, that I may tell you what will happen to you in days to come. [2]Assemble and hear, O sons of Jacob; listen to Israel your father. [3]Reuben, you are my firstborn, my might and the first fruits of my vigor, excelling in rank and excelling in power. [4]Unstable as water, you shall no longer excel because you went up onto your father's bed; then you defiled it—you went up onto my couch!

[5]Simeon and Levi are brothers; weapons of violence are their swords. [6]May I never come into their council; may I not be joined to their company— for in their anger they killed men, and at their whim they hamstrung oxen. [7]Cursed be their anger, for it is fierce, and their wrath, for it is cruel! I will divide them in Jacob, and scatter them in Israel.

[8]Judah, your brothers shall praise you; your hand shall be on the neck of your enemies; your father's sons shall bow down before you. [9]Judah is a lion's whelp; from the prey, my son, you have gone up. He crouches down, he stretches out like a lion, like a lioness—who dares rouse him up? [10]The scepter shall not depart from Judah, nor the ruler's staff from between his feet, until tribute comes to him; and the obedience of the peoples is his. [11]Binding his foal to the vine and his donkey's colt to the choice vine, he washes his garments in wine and his robe in the blood of grapes; [12]his eyes are darker than wine, and his teeth whiter than milk.

¹³Zebulun shall settle at the shore of the sea; he shall be a haven for ships, and his border shall be at Sidon. ¹⁴Issachar is a strong donkey, lying down between the sheepfolds; ¹⁵he saw that a resting place was good, and that the land was pleasant; so he bowed his shoulder to the burden, and became a slave at forced labor. ¹⁶Dan shall judge his people as one of the tribes of Israel. ¹⁷Dan shall be a snake by the roadside, a viper along the path, that bites the horse's heels so that its rider falls backward. ¹⁸I wait for your salvation, O LORD. ¹⁹Gad shall be raided by raiders, but he shall raid at their heels. ²⁰Asher's food shall be rich, and he shall provide royal delicacies. ²¹Naphtali is a doe let loose that bears lovely fawns.

²²Joseph is a fruitful bough, a fruitful bough by a spring; his branches run over the wall. ²³The archers fiercely attacked him; they shot at him and pressed him hard. ²⁴Yet his bow remained taut, and his arms were made agile by the hands of the Mighty One of Jacob, by the name of the Shepherd, the Rock of Israel, ²⁵by the God of your father, who will help you, by the Almighty who will bless you with blessings of heaven above, blessings of the deep that lies beneath, blessings of the breasts and of the womb. ²⁶The blessings of your father are stronger than the blessings of the eternal mountains, the bounties of the everlasting hills; may they be on the head of Joseph, on the brow of him who was set apart from his brothers. ²⁷Benjamin is a ravenous wolf, in the morning devouring the prey, and at evening dividing the spoil."

²⁸All these are the twelve tribes of Israel, and this is what their father said to them when he blessed them, blessing each one of them with a suitable blessing.

²⁹Then he charged them, saying to them, "I am about to be gathered to my people. Bury me with my ancestors—in the cave in the field of Ephron the Hittite, ³⁰in the cave in the field at Machpelah, near Mamre, in the land of Canaan, in the field that Abraham bought from Ephron the Hittite as a burial site. ³¹There Abraham and his wife Sarah were buried; there Isaac and his wife Rebekah were buried; and there I buried Leah— ³²the field and the cave that is in it were purchased from the Hittites." ³³When Jacob ended his charge to his sons, he drew up his feet into the bed, breathed his last, and was gathered to his people.

Reflection

At the end of his life, Father Jacob calls his twelve sons together and offers each one of them his paternal blessing. This blessing is not in every case what we would term a "blessing," for the father knows his sons well, predicts their characteristic future, and in a few cases foreshadows villainy and even punishment.

Naturally, he blesses Joseph (of the Coat of Many Colors) and prognosticates a fruitful future for that long-suffering heir. Jacob also blesses Judah. He envisions a somewhat mixed future for the others, except Reuben, who "shall not have pre-eminence"—and for a specific cause. He also sees his youngest son, Benjamin, as a "ravenous wolf."

In other words, Jacob's blessing on his sons is a mixed one. The father sees the reality of his sons and therefore understands that their futures will hinge on their temperament and character.

If you are a father or a mother, think about this for a minute: sometimes you see things in your children that you wish weren't there. Maybe a certain trait was visible, a little, when they were small. But in time it will become large, maybe even crippling.

Similarly, if you have a sibling or siblings, incipient childhood characteristics can grow as your sister or brother mature—and what was once a small thing has become disturbing.

Jacob's blessing of his twelve sons in this chapter of Genesis rings true. As a parent, you rejoice in the child's successes, as in the case of Judah and Joseph. You also hang your head low when the child "messes up," as is the case with Reuben. The human family is mixed. This will never change, short of the coming kingdom of God. Pray now for the afflicted and the afflicting ones in your family circle. God can "restore our fortunes…like the watercourses of the Negev" (Psalm 126:5).

— The Very Rev. Paul Zahl

Questions

Does your nuclear family reflect the mix that Jacob saw in his children? How so?

Are you at peace concerning the way your children's or your siblings' lives are turning out? If not, have you prayed specifically for the one about whom you are most concerned today?

Prayer

Dear God, help me accept the mixed condition of my immediate family. Help me also to pray concretely about the son/daughter/ brother/sister/other loved one for whom my heart is stressed today. Through Jesus Christ our Lord. *Amen.*

Genesis 50

50 Then Joseph threw himself on his father's face and wept over him and kissed him. ²Joseph commanded the physicians in his service to embalm his father. So the physicians embalmed Israel; ³they spent forty days in doing this, for that is the time required for embalming. And the Egyptians wept for him seventy days. ⁴When the days of weeping for him were past, Joseph addressed the household of Pharaoh, "If now I have found favor with you, please speak to Pharaoh as follows: ⁵My father made me swear an oath; he said, 'I am about to die. In the tomb that I hewed out for myself in the land of Canaan, there you shall bury me.' Now therefore let me go up, so that I may bury my father; then I will return." ⁶Pharaoh answered,

"Go up, and bury your father, as he made you swear to do."

⁷So Joseph went up to bury his father. With him went up all the servants of Pharaoh, the elders of his household, and all the elders of the land of Egypt, ⁸as well as all the household of Joseph, his brothers, and his father's household. Only their children, their flocks, and their herds were left in the land of Goshen. ⁹Both chariots and charioteers went up with him. It was a very great company. ¹⁰When they came to the threshing floor of Atad, which is beyond the Jordan, they held there a very great and sorrowful lamentation; and he observed a time of mourning for his father seven days. ¹¹When the Canaanite inhabitants of the land saw the mourning on the threshing floor of Atad, they said, "This is a grievous

mourning on the part of the Egyptians." Therefore the place was named Abel-mizraim; it is beyond the Jordan. [12]Thus his sons did for him as he had instructed them. [13]They carried him to the land of Canaan and buried him in the cave of the field at Machpelah, the field near Mamre, which Abraham bought as a burial site from Ephron the Hittite. [14]After he had buried his father, Joseph returned to Egypt with his brothers and all who had gone up with him to bury his father.

[15]Realizing that their father was dead, Joseph's brothers said, "What if Joseph still bears a grudge against us and pays us back in full for all the wrong that we did to him?" [16]So they approached Joseph, saying, "Your father gave this instruction before he died, [17]'Say to Joseph: I beg you, forgive the crime of your brothers and the wrong they did in harming you.' Now therefore please forgive the crime of the servants of the God of your father." Joseph wept when they spoke to him. [18]Then his brothers also wept, fell down before him, and said, "We are here as your slaves." [19]But Joseph said to them, "Do not be afraid! Am I in the place of God? [20]Even though you intended to do harm to me, God intended it for good, in order to preserve a numerous people, as he is doing today. [21]So have no fear; I myself will provide for you and your little ones." In this way he reassured them, speaking kindly to them.

[22]So Joseph remained in Egypt, he and his father's household; and Joseph lived one hundred ten years. [23]Joseph saw Ephraim's children of the third generation; the children of Machir son of Manasseh were also born on Joseph's knees. [24]Then Joseph said to his brothers, "I am about to die; but God will surely come to you, and bring you up out of this land to the land that he

swore to Abraham, to Isaac, and to Jacob." 25So Joseph made the Israelites swear, saying, "When God comes to you, you shall carry up my bones from here."

26And Joseph died, being one hundred ten years old; he was embalmed and placed in a coffin in Egypt.

Reflection

The final chapter of Genesis recounts the death of Joseph, whose acute sufferings had made him "a man of suffering and acquainted with infirmity" (Isaiah 53:3). God had saved Joseph twice in his bleakest hours, but Joseph had also assimilated unfairness and unjust punishment to the core of his soul.

In Chapter 50, Joseph's brothers are afraid of him, because he is returning to Canaan to bury his (and their) father. Their fear: that Joseph still "bears a grudge against us and pays us back in full for all the wrong that we did to him?" (Genesis 50:15).

Now comes the wonderful part of this concluding chapter in the first book of the Bible. Joseph says to his brothers, "Do not be afraid… Even though you intended to do harm to me, God intended it for good" (50:20). Joseph forgives his devious, conspiring brothers— for the second time. (He had forgiven them earlier, in Egypt, in Chapter 45.)

Joseph not only refuses to judge his brothers for what they did to him but also he cedes to God the ultimate causality of it. Joseph believes that by causing (through their crime) the families of Israel to settle in Egypt, God saves them from famine and begins a process of exile and restoration that will culminate in the Passover and the parting of the Red Sea.

Joseph visualizes everything—and in particular, the hard parts, the wicked parts of life—as under the hand of God. He has a very high idea of God's Providence. He sees God's backstory behind our front story. Joseph refuses to pass judgment on his brothers because he observes their cruelty as a part of God's saving plan for their descendants.

For me, the words of Genesis 50:20 are a high point of the Bible. They connect our pain with the presence and purpose of God. This can be a hard pill to swallow.

But when you are thrown into the pit of life, as Joseph was, or been lied about, as Joseph was, or entirely forgotten for years on end, as Joseph was; or been thrust into a stressful job that is not in your "pay grade," as Joseph was, you have a few choices: you can wallow and bemoan your predicament, or you can follow in Joseph's path, opening yourself to a "God's Eye" view of life.

The director Alfred Hitchcock occasionally would lift the camera high above the action to give the audience a big picture of the crime or significant plot-development. Like Hitchcock's "God's Eye" movement of his camera, Joseph offers an example of seeing the Big Picture—and invites us to do the same.

— **The Very Rev. Paul Zahl**

Questions

Has the "God's-Eye" of Joseph's words to his brothers ever been given to you? If so, when?

What effect did this insight into God's overriding purpose have on your conduct at the time? And how long did the insight last? Did it evanesce when outward circumstances improved?

Prayer

Dear God, there is something in my life that seems unfair and cruel. I'm bitter, to tell you the truth, at so-and-so and such-and-such. I'm bitter even at you. Why did you let that happen? Why did you not intervene in that terrible situation? Could you help me, like Joseph, to see your hand in the bad things and in the bad times.? Would you comfort me with your presence and plan? In your time, reveal the good to me. Reconcile me with the outcome of my life. Give me a glimpse of the good you intend even when others want to hurt me. Give me Joseph's view at the end of his life. Through Jesus Christ our Lord. *Amen.*

Afterword

Genesis. The very word evokes our imagination and invites our questions: "Where do we come from? Why are we here?" While we rightfully look to the sciences for answers to many of our queries, we as persons of faith can also turn to the scriptures that have formed and informed us to explore spiritually profound matters of purpose and meaning. The first of those biblical books, quite possibly the most well-known to most people, dives right into these deep waters.

As you have found in your Bible Challenge study of Genesis—whether it was new to you or very familiar—the book speaks of beginnings, origins, first things, and the Source of life itself. Genesis 1:1 says it like this: "In the beginning, God created the heavens and the earth." Now, take an even more focused look at those initial words: "In the beginning, God."

However we understand the details of creation, the particulars of life and its processes in all its myriad forms, the deeper truth is that God is and always has been at the very heart of it all. We are introduced to many fascinating characters in Genesis—Adam and Eve, Cain and Abel, Noah, Abraham and Sarah, Isaac and Rebecca, Jacob whose name is changed to Israel, his spouses and sons, and Joseph, who paves the way for the events of Exodus, the next book in the Torah. Yet, all these are supporting players who make their way across the stage, while the primary figure in every scene is God. Indeed, God is the loving, liberating, life-giving one who both guides them and walks beside them in all their various stories, the one who is both their source and their strength.

We can take heart that this same God guides and walks beside us now. We who are followers of Jesus of Nazareth know that the opening words of Genesis are echoed in another of our biblical books: "In the beginning was the Word, and the Word was with God, and the Word was God." And further along in that passage from the first chapter of John's Gospel, we read that "the Word became flesh and lived among us." When we look at Jesus in the gospels, when we hear his teachings and see his sacrifice, we are continually reminded that God is love.

Genesis. The biblical book and the very word evoke our imagination and invite our questions: "Where do we come from?" From God… who is love itself. "Why are we here?" Because of God…who is love itself. Now, our calling, our purpose, our reason for continuing on this journey of ours is nothing less than to love as God has loved us. As I have preached in countless places, if it's not about love, it's not about God. The good news from Genesis onward is that Love was there at creation's birth, Love was there at Abraham's calling, and Love is here with you and me now.

The Most Rev. Michael Bruce Curry
XXVII Presiding Bishop of the Episcopal Church

W. Frank Allen has served as rector of St. David's (Radnor) Church in the Diocese of Pennsylvania since 1997. In God's service, the church he serves has grown spiritually and physically and has developed deep and lasting partnerships in the region and in the world to feed, clothe, house, care for, and educate thousands of God's children. Frank is the author of the *Spiritual Gifts Project*, has served on the board of Gathering of Leaders, St. James School, Invite Welcome Connect, and Duke Divinity School. He and his wife, Amy, have three grown sons and one grandson. *Days 47 and 48*

Dane E. Boston is the dean of Trinity Episcopal Cathedral in Columbia, South Carolina. He and his wife, Debby, are graduates of Washington and Lee University, and they are blessed with four beautiful children. Dane studied for holy orders at Yale Divinity School and served parishes in Greenwich, Connecticut, and Cooperstown, New York, before his call to Trinity. *Days 37 and 38*

Mark Francisco Bozzuti-Jones is an Episcopal priest at Trinity Church Wall Street in New York City. He has served as director for pastoral care and senior clergy for partnerships in Latin America and the Caribbean and presently is the priest and director for spiritual formation at Trinity Retreat Center in West Cornwall, Connecticut. He is Jamaican and a former Roman Catholic Jesuit priest. Mark's intellectual interests include the impact of social issues on faith and spirituality, race relations, the economic plight of the poor in Third World countries, and liturgical renewal with a focus on diversity and recognizing the gifts of children. He is an award-winning author;

recent books include *Face to the Rising Sun: Reflections on Spirituals and Justice; God Created; Jesus the Word; The Gospel of Barack Hussein Obama According to Mark; The Rastafari Book of Common Prayer;* and *Absalom Jones: America's First Black Priest. Day 24*

Grace Pritchard Burson is a priest, doula, writer, and farmer. She was ordained in the Episcopal Diocese of New Hampshire and now serves as the incumbent of the Anglican Church of All Saints by the Lake in Dorval, Quebec. She has written for *Fidelia's Sisters* (the blog of Young Clergy Women International) and for *Earth & Altar Magazine* and was recently part of a team of four priests in the Anglican Church of Canada who "translated" Forward Movement's *Walk in Love*, a guide to the Episcopal Church, into a Canadian context entitled *To Love and Serve. Days 5 and 6*

Justin E. Crisp is associate rector and theologian-in-residence at St. Mark's Episcopal Church in New Canaan, Connecticut, and lecturer in Anglican Studies at Berkeley Divinity School at Yale. A pastor at heart, he is captivated by what God has done for us in Christ and loves bringing the wisdom of 2,000 years of attempts to be faithful to Jesus to bear on the predicaments of life, perennial and modern. He is co-editor with Miroslav Volf of *Joy and Human Flourishing: Essays on Theology, Culture, and the Good Life* (2015) and is working on two books, the first an intervention in the theology of sexuality and the second a pastoral guide to the problem of evil. *Days 3 and 4*

Michael Bruce Curry is the twenty-seventh presiding bishop and primate of the Episcopal Church. At the church's 78th General Convention in June 2015, he was elected to a nine-year term in this role and installed in November of that year; he serves as the

Episcopal Church's chief pastor, spokesperson, and president and chief executive officer. Throughout his ministry, Bishop Curry has been a prophetic leader, particularly in the areas of racial reconciliation, climate change, evangelism, immigration policy, and marriage equality. The animating vision and message of his ministry is Jesus of Nazareth and his way of radical, sacrificial love, and he regularly reminds Episcopalians they are "the Episcopal branch of the Jesus Movement." *Afterword*

Alberto R. Cutié is the rector of Saint Benedict's Episcopal Church, a diverse and dynamic parish located in Plantation, Florida. Alberto is a well-known and popular radio and television talk show host in the Latino world, where he deals with everyday issues impacting our society. His website is padrealberto.com. *Days 13 and 14*

Ryan Fleenor serves as rector of Saint Luke's Parish in Darien, Connecticut. A native North Carolinian, he studied history at the University of Virginia and earned his master of divinity degree at Yale Divinity School. Prior to Saint Luke's, he served for 10 years at St. James' Church, Madison Avenue, in New York City, most recently as vicar. He also serves on the boards of Forward Movement and the Episcopal Church at Yale. *Days 43 and 44*

J. Malone Gilliam serves as the rector of St. George's Episcopal Church in Nashville, Tennessee. He has previously served congregations in Edenton, North Carolina, and Sullivan's Island, South Carolina. Malone and his wife, Mary, have four daughters. *Days 19 and 20*

A Journey through Genesis

Peter S. Hawkins is professor emeritus of religion and literature at Yale's Divinity School, Berkeley Divinity School, and Institute of Sacred Music. From 2000-2008, he directed the Scripture and Literary Arts program at Boston University. His work as a teacher and writer has long focused on the "Divine Comedy" in *Dante's Testaments: Essays in Scriptural Imagination, Dante: A Brief History, The Poets' Dante: Twentieth-Century Reflections, Undiscovered Country: Imagining the World to Come.* A frequent contributor of *The Christian Century,* his work on scripture can be seen in *Scrolls of Love: Ruth and the Song of Songs and From the Margins I: Women in the Hebrew Bible and their Afterlives.* He has also published on contemporary American fiction in the Listening for God series (with Paula Carlson) and in *The Bible and the American Short Story* (with Lesleigh Cushing Stahlberg). *Days 15 and 16*

Mitchell M. Hurvitz (Rabbi Mitch) has served Temple Sholom of Greenwich, Connecticut, since 1995. He is a noted scholar, teacher, religious and social activist, and preacher. A frequent guest speaker at synagogues and churches, study groups, community institutions, and universities, Rabbi Mitch is charismatic, engages individuals, and stimulates hearts and minds. An author of numerous popular and scholarly articles, he has also written the "Introduction to the Jewish Faith" and the *Encyclopedia of Judaism* for publisher Facts on File. He is the co-founder of The Shalom Center for Interfaith Learning & Fellowship. *Days 1 and 2*

Brenda G. Husson retired in 2023 as rector of St. James' Church in New York City, New York, having served there for more than 26 years. Ordained in the Diocese of Central New York, prior to her call to St. James', she served in various roles at All Angels' Church on the Upper West Side of Manhattan, Grace Church, White Plains, New York, and St. John's Church, New City, all within the Diocese of New York. She also served as director of the Episcopal Evangelical Education Society. A graduate of Union Theological Seminary in New York City, she and her husband Thomas Faulkner, sculptor and Episcopal priest, now make their home on Cape Cod together with their beloved dogs. *Days 33 and 34*

W. Nicholas Knisely is the thirteenth bishop of the Episcopal Diocese of Rhode Island. He formerly served as a priest in Arizona, Bethlehem, Pittsburgh, and Delaware. He has authored or contributed to several devotional books and is an active blogger online at *Entangled States.* He is active in conversations about the intersection of faith and science nationally and internationally. *Days 25 and 26*

Lucinda Laird is the retired dean of the American Cathedral in Paris and has also served as rector as St. Matthew's, Louisville, Kentucky, and St. Mark's, Teaneck, New Jersey. It took very little time for her to realize that retirement did not agree with her, so she has now begun a position as chaplain (or vicar) of St. George's Anglican Church in Venice, Italy. *Days 45 and 46*

Eric H. F. Law is the founder of the Kaleidoscope Institute, which provides resources to equip leaders to create diverse and sustainable communities. He is the author of many books, including *Holy Currencies, Fear Not: Living Grace and Truth in a Frightened World,* and *The Wolf Shall Dwell with the Lamb.* He is a singer-songwriter-recording artist, an Episcopal priest, a photographer, and a playwright. Listen to his music at: erichflaw.hearnow.com. *Day 28*

Lynne Jordal Martin works for a major news organization. A passionate Education for Ministry mentor, she serves on the vestry of Trinity Church Wall Street where she is chair of the Grants Committee. She lives with her family in Westchester County, New York, and worships at Christ Church in Greenwich, Connecticut. *Days 9 and 10*

Gregory S. Marx is the senior rabbi of Congregation Beth Or in Maple Glen, Pennsylvania. He has served this community for nearly 34 years. He is a staunch advocate for Bible study, social action, and interfaith dialogue. *Days 17 and 18*

Andrew McGowan is dean of the Berkeley Divinity School and McFaddin Professor of Anglican Studies at Yale University in New Haven, Connecticut. An Australian Anglican priest, he was formerly warden of Trinity College at The University of Melbourne. His work on biblical and early Christian texts and practices has appeared in leading journals and in his books, including *Ascetic Eucharists: Food and Drink in Early Christian Ritual Meals* and *Ancient Christian Worship*. He is also the author of *Seven Last Words: Cross and Creation*. *Days 21 and 22*

Jeffrey W. Mello serves as the sixteenth bishop of The Episcopal Church in Connecticut. He was elected in May of 2022 and consecrated in October of the same year. Prior to ordination to the priesthood, he worked in the psychiatry department of Massachusetts General Hospital as a clinical social worker. Jeffrey grew up at church camp in Rhode Island and continues to find God while eating s'mores around a campfire under a blanket of stars. *Days 41 and 42*

Gregory Mobley is an ordained American Baptist minister and a professor of the Hebrew Bible at Andover Newton Seminary at Yale Divinity School. Among his books on the Bible are *The Return of the Chaos Monsters—and Other Backstories of the Bible, The Empty Men: The Heroic Tradition of Ancient Israel,* and with co-author T. J. Wray, *The Birth of Satan: Tracing the Devil's Biblical Roots.* Gregory is also active in interreligious learning and interfaith dialogue and co-edited *My Neighbor's Faith: Stories of Interreligious Encounter, Growth, and Transformation. Days 31 and 32*

Jessica Schaap is missioner of Christian formation for the Diocese of New Westminster, Vancouver, Canada, on the traditional unceded lands of the Coast Salish peoples. Jessica works for the Diocese of New Westminster to equip and encourage parishes of all sizes and people of all ages to grow in Christian understanding and faith. She finds incredible joy in witnessing people have new hope and know a closer relationship with God. She has been an Anglican priest for 14 years and prior to becoming a missioner, she was an assistant priest and rector in downtown Vancouver. Outside of work, she loves to birdwatch, cook, garden, read poetry, and go for walks. She longs for the day when Christ is all in all. *Day 23*

Eva Suarez serves as the canon for community engagement at the Cathedral of St. John the Divine, in New York City. She is passionate about discipleship and the ways people can grow in faith through service to others.. *Days 35 and 36*

Christine Trainor is the senior priest of the Anglican Church in the Emirate of Abu Dhabi, United Arab Emirates. She has served in 12 congregations in the Episcopal and Anglican churches, including St. Bartholomew's Church in New York City, Grace Cathedral in

San Francisco, and St. Paul's Cathedral in London. A graduate of Yale University Divinity School, she has written and contributed to eleven books on preaching, enriching prayer, and reading Holy Scripture critically and faithfully. She has won scholarships and awards for her preaching and recently participated in the Interfaith Alliance advising the G20 conference in 2023, as a panelist hosted by the Muslim Council of Elders, and keynoted a conference for children, youth, and educators across the region from South India to Turkey. *Days 39 and 40*

Winnie Varghese is the 23rd rector of St. Luke's, Atlanta. She has done other things in the church but for right now is delighted by the congregation of St. Luke's and her family and dogs. *Day 27*

Marek P. Zabriskie serves as rector of Christ Church in Greenwich, Connecticut, and has served churches in Nashville, Tennessee, Richmond, Virginia, and Fort Washington, Pennsylvania. He is the founder and director of The Bible Challenge and the Center for Biblical Studies (www.thecenterforbiblicalstudies.org), which freely promotes and shares The Bible Challenge around the world. More than a million Anglicans have participated in it. He has hiked over 2,000 miles across Spain and Portugal and is an honorary canon at the Anglican Cathedral of the Redeemer in Madrid. He has edited 11 books in The Bible Challenge series and is the author of *Doing the Bible Better: The Bible Challenge and the Transformation of the Episcopal Church. Days 11 and 12*

Paul Zahl is a retired Episcopal minister. He served parishes in Silver Spring, Maryland; New York City and Westchester County in New York; Charleston, South Carolina; Birmingham, Alabama; and Chevy Chase, Maryland. He was also dean/president of Trinity

(Episcopal) School for Ministry in Ambridge, Pennyslvania. Paul and his wife, Mary, have three grown sons, all of whom are in Christian service, and seven grandchildren. They live in Winter Garden, Florida, and Greenwich, Connecticut. *Days 49 and 50*

Becky Zartman is the canon for evangelism and formation at Christ Church Cathedral in Houston, Texas, and often collaborates with Lifelong Learning at Virginia Theological Seminary. She is the co-editor of *Belovedness: Finding God (and Self) on Campus,* a book written by college chaplains for graduating high school seniors and college students. *Days 29 and 30*

Dwight Zscheile is vice president of innovation and professor of congregational mission and leadership at Luther Seminary in St. Paul, Minnesota. An Episcopal priest, his books include *Leading Faithful Innovation* (with Michael Binder and Tessa Pinkstaff), *The Agile Church*, and *People of the Way: Renewing Episcopal Identity.* His work focuses on helping Christian communities connect more deeply with God, each other, and their neighbors. *Days 7 and 8*

Forward Movement is committed to inspiring disciples and empowering evangelists. We live out our ministry through publishing books, daily reflections, studies for small groups, and online resources.

Hundreds of thousands of people read our daily devotions through *Forward Day by Day*, which is also available in Spanish (*Adelante Día a Día*) and Braille, online, as a podcast, and as an app for your smartphones or tablets. We actively seek partners across the church and look for ways to provide resources that inspire and challenge.

A ministry of the Episcopal Church since 1935, Forward Movement is a nonprofit organization funded by sales of resources and gifts from generous donors. To learn more, visit forwardmovement.org.